THE
CONSTITUTION
OF A
GREAT
LEADER

LEADERSHIP *in*
the 21*st* CENTURY

THE CONSTITUTION *OF A* GREAT LEADER

LEADERSHIP *in the* 21*st* CENTURY

CEVIN ORMOND

Editors: Jordan Thames and Joshua Owens
Cover Design: John M. Lucas
Interior Design: mycustombookcover.com

Indigo River Publishing
3 West Garden Street, Ste. 352
Pensacola, FL 32502
www.indigoriverpublishing.com

Ordering Information:
Quantity sales: Special discounts are available on quantity purchases by corporations, associations, and others. For details, contact the publisher at the address above.

Orders by US trade bookstores and wholesalers: Please contact the publisher at the address above.

Printed in the United States of America

Library of Congress Control Number: 2019940074

ISBN: 978-1-948080-90-3

First Edition

With Indigo River Publishing, you can always expect great books, strong voices, and meaningful messages. Most importantly, you'll always find . . . *words worth reading.*

TABLE OF CONTENTS

Introduction

‿❧

On November 26, 1971, in Portland, Oregon, I raised my arm and repeated the following words:

"I, Cevin Ormond, do solemnly swear (or affirm) that I will support and defend the Constitution of the United States against all enemies, foreign and domestic; that I will bear true faith and allegiance to the same; and that I will obey the orders of the President of the United States and the orders of the officers appointed over me, according to regulations and the Uniform Code of Military Justice. So help me God."

Then I got on a bus to the airport and flew to San Antonio, Texas, to begin United States Air Force Basic Training. I was 20 years old, recently married with a newly pregnant wife, and had no clue where this one act would take me.

Up until that time I had never been outside the western United States, except for a couple trips to Tijuana, Mexico. I graduated from high school in American Falls, Idaho, and began working as a butcher (my father's profession for over

40 years). I had a few college credits under my belt, but no real career direction beyond cutting meat. Although I didn't really have any direction yet, I did know that I didn't want to be a butcher for the rest of my life.

As the oldest of eight children at the time (there are now ten of us) I had some level of leadership responsibility forced upon me, but I knew very little about how to lead effectively. I had been taught how to work hard, and I was, and still am, grateful for that, but you can't teach what you don't know, and my parents didn't know much about leadership. As a result, I had no clue of its crucial role in success.

You see, every organization, from an individual life to an entire country, can be modeled and thought of as a three-legged stool.

The first leg is the Technical Leg. This is what you do. For example, I was a meat cutter, then I was trained in electronics in the Air Force and I fixed radio equipment. After I was discharged from the Air Force, I went to the University of Washington and graduated in Electrical Engineering, so I became an electrical engineer. Later, I got my executive MBA from the University of Utah. Now, I am a leadership expert, a professional speaker, an actor, a bestselling author, and a credibility coach.

Here's the thing. I said "I am" all these things, but that's not technically true (although that is how most of us speak about our profession). The fact is, those things are actually what I do, not what I am. They represent the technical aspects of my professional life, but say nothing about why I do what I do. These things represent the Technical Leg of my three-legged stool.

The second leg is the Management Leg. I mentioned

my MBA, so I have been trained to manage and have done so extensively for over thirty-five years. Management is about systems and how we deal with things – time, money, equipment, and various other resources.

The third leg of the stool is the Leadership Leg. This leg is about how we deal with people and is the most important of the three legs. People can't be managed–although that's often what it's called–but they can, and must, be led and led effectively for any organization to be successful.

The thing is that most people, businesses, government (and other) organizations are missing either one or two of these legs, and a three-legged stool that is missing even one leg is not stable! It will very easily fall over, and trying to stay upright with fewer than three legs will consume all your time, effort, and resources, which means there are no resources available for growth and progress.

The missing leg is almost never the Technical Leg. That one is usually just fine. Too often people focus all their energy there when they or their organizations aren't thriving, but that is rarely, if ever, the problem, and so the issues persist.

Sometimes the missing leg is the Management Leg, but strengthening that leg is usually a relatively easy fix. It's a matter of adding and refining systems like finances, production, delivery, etc. It's usually a pretty straightforward process.

The missing, or weakest, leg is almost always the Leadership Leg, and there are several reasons for this. First, leadership is not very well understood by most people. Second, too many people think they understand it, so they stop learning and working to improve their leadership skills. Third, leadership skills can't be trained but must be developed. This is an experiential process and not primarily intellectual like developing technical and management skills, so developing leadership is a much slower and less visible process. Too many people are unwilling to invest the time and effort required.

So why should you read this book? What's in it for you?

If you want to fix the problems in your business, your organization, and your life, you must develop better leadership skills, first in yourself and then in others around you. Only then can you grow that third leg and gain the stability that you are looking for. But you must develop your leadership based upon true principles that are proven to always work. Otherwise, you will never get the success you desire in whatever aspect of your life or your work you're struggling with.

I can guarantee that if you implement the principles discussed in this book that things will improve for you over time. There is no quick fix, but these things work! I know because they have worked and continue to work for me, and I'm no different than you in any significant way. If they work for me (and they do!), they will work for you, too.

So now here I am – decades later – speaking, writing, coaching, and training people all over the world on the amazing leadership principles embedded within the Constitution that I swore an oath to uphold and defend all those years ago. Interestingly enough, learning and practicing those very leadership principles contained in the Constitution have fundamentally and permanently altered my constitution – who and what I am – in ways that I could have never imagined back then.

My hope is that, by sharing some of my story that you can learn from my mistakes and not have to make them all yourself. Then we can examine the timeless principles and learn how to use the wisdom embedded within two separate constitutions—the Constitution of the United States and the constitution that makes up a great leader. By studying the ideals that these two constitutions share, we will discover how they can impact, alter, and improve every organization in the 21st century and guarantee that you and your organizations will thrive.

Section I: Leadership, Constitutions, and True Principles

Two Constitutions, One
Set of Principles

❧

What to learn:
What makes a principle a "true principle"?
Why is it critical to successful leadership to operate using true principles?
Where can true principles be found?
The three "C's" of great leadership – the basis of your personal constitution as a leader.

What to avoid:
Intellectual understanding instead of actual practice and internal growth.

Since 1989 I have been a full-time professional speaker, and that's how I've earned most of my income – getting paid to speak. As a kid, my teachers were constantly telling me to be quiet. The good news is that now I can earn more in a one-hour speech than they could make in two months, which, I must admit, is a great feeling. The bad news is that I can't afford to be sick. The show must go on, and when I have been hired to speak I always show up, stand, and deliver. I'm proud to say I have *never* missed a speech. There have definitely been times when I would much rather have been in bed than on stage, but I have always given my very best to my audience and I always will. That's my promise to those who hire me. Luckily, I have a strong constitution.

I'm sure you're familiar with different variations of the phrase, "I almost never get sick, I guess I just have a really strong constitution." What people mean by that, of course, is that they are healthy and their immune system works well. So how come they have such a strong constitution? It's likely a combination of two things – their genetic endowment (the healthy body they were born with), and the things they do to take care of their body (exercise, adequate rest, proper nutrition, etc.). In other words, their makeup, or basic framework, and their actions work together to create that "strong constitution". So why do they choose those particular actions? They are choosing to behave in a way consistent with true principles—true principles of health in this case. We all know these principles of health because they're blasted at us from all directions so incessantly that it's impossible not to hear them almost every day. Besides that, we all know them almost intuitively. We instinctively know the things we should be doing to take care of and improve our health.

While just knowing something is all well and good, that's not the test of true principles. Human perception can be manipulated, but true principles have two special characteristics. First, true principles always work – they worked yesterday, they work today, and they will continue to work in the future. Second, they also don't care what anybody thinks about them. In other words, they aren't affected by opinion or belief.

I often use the example of gravity. Gravity is a true principle. If I hold a pen or some other object in my hand and I let it go, it *always* falls down. It never falls up, it never just hovers, it falls down. That was true yesterday, it's true today, it will be true tomorrow, and gravity doesn't care if you believe in it or not. It just does its thing anyway. You can say you don't believe in gravity, and you may even be able to convince yourself that you don't believe in gravity, but if you step off of a building gravity doesn't care what you believe. You will fall downward until you hit the ground. Period. No exceptions (do not try this at home or anywhere else).

So, if your physical constitution is a function of a good framework and the effects of the true principles you incorporate into your life, the same can be said of your constitution as a leader. You need a solid structural framework and true leadership principles that you practice and incorporate into your life. That's the first constitution we are talking about.

The second Constitution is the Constitution of the United States of America, the oldest Constitution in the world. All other written Constitutions came later and are patterned after it. So why is that the case? Why is it still around and working after all these years, and why have so many other countries copied it?

The answer is pretty simple, really, and it's because the Constitution of the United States of America is based upon a structural framework that embodies true leadership principles throughout the entirety of the document. It was a product of the environment that shaped the principles of the Framers of the Constitution. You see, true leadership principles are not new; they were around and functioning long before the Constitution was written. The Constitution, however, was the first governing document that acted as an embodiment of these principles. And, of course, since it is based upon true principles, it has functioned well since its formal adoption on March 4, 1789, and continues to function well today - regardless of anyone's opinion about it. Just a side note: I said that it has functioned well – not perfectly. That's why we have the amendment processes.

What I find fascinating is that, while I have found many things written about the Constitution from both legal and historical perspectives, I have not found anything about the Constitution from a leadership point of view. I find that particularly sad, and think that we are missing the boat by not looking at it this way. After all, these true principles have been working for over 200 years. So, if we apply them properly, they will continue to work for us as leaders in all aspects of our lives. Everyone is a leader at some level, so these principles can help everyone who uses them.

Imagine what you can accomplish when you are mentored by the likes of Washington, Franklin, Jefferson, and Adams! Where will that take you and your organization, your family, and your life? While these men were not perfect (as nobody ever is), they were without doubt some of the greatest leaders the world has ever produced. I can't think of a finer group of mentors, or of a more incredible mastermind to work with. If we think about the true leadership principles they embodied, we can see that they were decisive, loyal, courageous, clear thinking, intensely focused, long-term thinkers, and passionate dreamers. If it's true (and I'm certain it is) that you become the average of the five people you hang out with the most, then I, for one, want to hang out with people like them. Since I can't hang out with them face-to-face, for obvious reasons, I'll do the next best thing and hang out with their ideas, their writings, their principles, and their legacy.

This brings up a very important question that must be answered before we delve further. While we can all agree that the Framers were great leaders, since the results of their leadership are with us over two centuries later, what exactly is leadership, and what makes a great leader? Some people try to simplify the answer to that question by saying something like, "leadership is influence" or some similar, short tagline. While it's true that part of leadership is influence, leadership itself is much more global and multi-faceted than that, particularly great leadership. Leadership is something that is felt, not something that can be quickly or easily defined and categorized. The fact is you can *feel* a great leader. In other words, leadership (good or bad) is felt, not intellectually measured or observed. In fact, it has to be developed and cannot be trained. Development is a time-consuming process, and developing yourself into a great leader is the quest of a lifetime. In fact, it's actually a permanent lifestyle choice! If you want to develop great leadership in yourself, you must commit to improving your leadership every day for the rest of your life. If you make that choice, execute, do the work, and continue for the rest of your life with those efforts, the rewards are beyond imagination. The good news is that it starts bearing fruit reasonably soon – not instantly, but fairly soon. However, you must look carefully to see that progress, as the first signs are easy to miss. Jim Rohn used to talk about the law of the harvest, as did Paul Harvey and many others. It works like this:

Initially the farmer has to exercise faith as he (or she) plants seeds in the Spring. He invests a lot of time and money in this process based upon faith that he will receive a crop at the end of the season. He not only plants, but he waters the planted ground (an expensive and time-consuming process as well) even though nothing is visible above ground for many days after planting. He does this because he has faith in the process and faith that he planted good seeds. His faith is based in part on previous experience but, as any investor in the stock market knows, past performance is no guarantee of future performance. In the farmer's case, the crop could fail, he could have bad seeds, the weather could destroy the crop – any of a number of things could keep him from enjoying a bountiful harvest. But he keeps watering anyway, continues to invest more and more time and money into the potential crop, and almost every time he eventually sees shoots breaking through the surface of the soil. He still has to continue watering, cultivating, weeding, killing bugs, and all the rest (based upon faith) all the way up to the harvest, and then he has to harvest the crop in order for all that faith and effort to be rewarded. Then what does he do? He exercises faith once again and starts the process all over the next year.

Developing your leadership is a lot like that. After a while of working daily on your leadership principles, you will begin to see some of the "shoots" of your growing leadership poke their little heads above the ground and start to become visible in your life. Usually you aren't even the first one to see them. Often someone will make a comment that will surprise you and cause you to say, "Wow! I never even noticed that until they mentioned it but, I can see that I have made some progress." You can then build on that and certainly draw encouragement from the fact that your hard and consistent work is beginning to bear some fruit. It may be an improved relationship with a loved one that you notice first, or maybe a project at work, but whatever it is, notice it, embrace it, celebrate it, and promise yourself that you will continue your development process.

Another point about developing leadership is that because great leadership is felt, it is an emotional experience. And because language (at least in written form) is primarily an intellectual process, it is extremely difficult to effectively write about leadership is a way that clearly conveys the width, depth, breadth, and emotional experience of it. This is what I call "The Elephant Problem". This problem is outlined in a parable from India that was captured in a poem written by John Godfrey Saxe that begins as follows:

"It was six men of Indostan
To learning much inclined,
Who went to see the Elephant
(Though all of them were blind),
That each by observation
Might satisfy his mind"

The poem then goes on to describe how each of the six blind men touched a different part of the elephant, and based upon that limited one-touch experience assumed that he understood the entire elephant. One touched the side and thought it was like a wall. Another touched a tusk and thought it was like a spear and so on with each of the blind men. Then they proceeded to argue about the true nature of the elephant. While each was totally convinced he was right based upon his own personal experience, each one was partly right and each one was partly wrong because none had experienced the entire elephant, only a small part of it.

When it comes to leadership, we all suffer from The Elephant Problem for several reasons. First of all, great leadership is a pretty big elephant. It is possible to spend a lifetime learning more about it, practicing, and getting better. Second, leadership is not directly measurable. It's like the wind. While the wind clearly exists, you can't see it, only its effects. You can measure some aspects of the wind, such as its speed and direction, but that isn't really what the wind is. However, when you go outside and feel the power of the wind, you get a much better idea of what it is. Simple measurements can't convey the wind; it must be experienced to be understood. In fact, there are different types of wind, each of which has a unique quality about it that can only be understood through experience.

I really learned this lesson when I experienced my first tropical storm. During my time in the US Air Force, I was stationed at Anderson AFB, Guam. My job at that time was radio maintenance and I was selected for a world-wide deployment team. My task there was to insure that the communications equipment stayed up and running correctly. In typical military fashion, they gave me the full battery of immunizations so that I could be deployed anywhere in world on short notice and would be protected from the various diseases I might encounter. Then they deployed me twice - both times to Anderson South, about ten miles south of the main base, and both times during tropical storms. This was so that when the power and phone lines went out (which they always did) the commanders would still have communication with that area via radio, as this was long before the era of cell phones.

So, I was comfortably sleeping in my bunk one night, when around 1a.m. a dispatcher knocked on the door, woke me up, and told me I had to deploy. I dressed and stepped out into the night to the strangest wind I have ever experienced. The only way I can describe it is that the wind in that storm felt like the entire world was moving in one direction. Tropical cyclonic winds have an entirely different character than other winds. Once I experienced that wind, I never forgot it, and every time that I find myself in that type of wind it is instantly recognizable. I then proceed to get into a step-van (basically like a UPS van, except blue), load in the radio equipment and tools, pick up the radio operator, and the two of us head down to Anderson South at about 2 a.m. Thankfully I was driving, because the wind was strong enough that the van was leaning sideways. It was pitch dark (no street lights), I dodged flying coconuts, palm fronds, pieces of tin roof, and various other debris, with the poor radio operator sitting beside me scared to death and unable to do anything about it. I tried to calm him as much as possible, but nobody was happier when we arrived safely than he was!

The point of this story is that leadership, like the wind, must be experienced to be understood. Once great leadership is experienced, it is instantly recognizable when you find it again. However, this makes it difficult to communicate it in words since words are a left-brain quality, and emotions are experienced in the brain's limbic areas with assistance from the right-brain – places where words and language do not exist. This fact makes The Elephant Problem worse. Here's why:

Every leader, every aspiring leader, and every leadership expert (including me) only sees the leadership elephant based upon their experience with it. This means that no one ever learns it all, and everyone can learn and improve as a leader. Worse yet, even if someone did know it all, they would never be able to communicate everything with words. When I tell you a story, like I did above, your mind takes on the role of co-storyteller and you visualize your own experience. The picture you painted in your mind is most likely similar, but significantly different than the memory I have in my mind. Your experience blends with mine, and you become a co-creator of the story which you see, hear, and feel in your mind and heart. This fact is one part of how a good leader can enhance their charisma and create greater buy-in and engagement from their followers.

True Leadership Principle: Great leaders enhance their charisma by telling engaging stories constantly.

So, what are you supposed to do to deal with the double whammy of The Elephant Problem, and the fact that words are such a poor tool to communicate the essence of leadership? I'll get into that later. First there are a few other things that you need to understand.

LEADERSHIP VS. LEGAL AND HISTORICAL PERSPECTIVES

One question that always fascinates me is, "What has been missed or overlooked?" Another great question is, "Why has that thing been missed or overlooked?" This brings up another principle:

True Leadership Principle: Great answers are found by asking great questions. If you want to improve the quality of your answers you must improve the quality of the questions you are asking.

As I've looked at leadership over the years and noticed the principles upon which great leadership operates, I've also noticed where those principles are found and where they can be better learned and studied. One of those places, of course, is in the Constitution of the United States, since the true leadership principles in that document have been working successfully for such a long period of time.

The thing is, while I have seen many books written on the Constitution that come from a historical or a legal perspective, I am not aware of any that look at it from the perspective of the leadership principles it embodies. So I asked myself the questions above. In particular, why has so little been written about the leadership lessons contained in the Constitution? I'm not really sure what the answer to that question is, and I'm sure there are a number of reasons, but since it hasn't been properly examined there is certainly a need. It seems to me that if people understood those leadership lessons better, they would be able to lead better, and better leadership is the key to better relationships, better organizations, and a better world.

It also might just be that, because great leadership is my passion (and expertise), I simply view things from that perspective, just as a historian views all things historically, and an attorney views all things from a legal point of view. It's the same for all of us; we are all subject to selective perception. For example, as soon as you buy a new car, you suddenly start noticing cars everywhere of the same make, model, and color. The question is, did a bunch of people suddenly decide to buy a car like yours, or were they there all the time and you just started to notice? Of course they were always there, but now you see them everywhere. That's selective perception. I have been studying and practicing leadership for decades, so I see leadership principles everywhere. As you increase your leadership skills the same thing will happen to you. It's just human nature.

So, the next great question is, "What are the components of great leadership that I should be looking for?" In other words, how can you recognize great leadership beyond how it feels and seeing the long-term effects it produces? I find it helpful to break great leadership down into three parts which I call "The Three 'Cs' of Great Leadership" – Character, Conduct, and Charisma.

Character

Character is the number one component of great leadership, and anyone attempting to be a leader without good solid character is bound to fail eventually. Without good character, disaster is inevitable. There are many examples of leaders who were very charismatic and yet, because their character was bankrupt, they led themselves and their followers into disaster. One of the most notable examples of this was Adolph Hitler. Hitler was one of the best public speakers the world has ever known, and people often spoke about the electricity they felt in his presence. Just look up a video of him stirring up a crowd of a million people on YouTube to see what I mean. But his character defects caused the deaths of over 50 million people as a result of the war he started, World War II.

Seth Godin, marketing and leadership expert, entrepreneur, and multiple New York Times Bestselling Author, once said, "Choosing to develop character is difficult, because it requires avoiding the shorter, more direct path. It can be slow, expensive and difficult work. And rewarding character is difficult as well, because someone is probably offering you an alternative that's cheaper or faster. A sure road to a quick payday. But... Every time we avoid the easy in favor of what's right, we create ripples. Character begets more character, weaving together the fabric of our culture, the kind of world we'd rather live in."

There are many notable examples of people that are commonly viewed as leaders who created serious problems for themselves and others because of a flawed character. The problem with what they created is that, like anything leadership related, there are long-lasting and often unrecoverable effects from what they did. Too often these people and those who followed them have lost their livelihoods, money, relationships, their freedom, and sometimes even their lives. I refer to these people as "so called" or "apparent" leaders. While they were operating in a leadership role and had people, sometimes millions of people, following them, they were not great, or even good, leaders due to the serious shortfalls in their character. Many of these "so-called" leaders end up being impeached, imprisoned, or even killed as a result of the unfortunate decisions that they made, and their unwillingness to improve their character. Sadly, government, businesses, the media, and other organizations are full of these "so-called" leaders. Many even claim that character is unimportant, but they are gravely mistaken. Character counts, and it counts the most of the three "C's".

True Leadership Principle: Great character is the foundation of a great leader. Without character, true and lasting leadership is not possible, and your leadership will always fail eventually. There are only a few absolute barriers in life, things that restrict you from achievement, but this is one the most important of that group. If you want to lead effectively you MUST develop great character!

That being said it's important to remember that no one has perfect, unflawed character, but great leaders recognize its importance and work every day to enhance and improve their own. That's the critical point. Keep working and keep improving. You will never be perfect, but if you are a little closer to that perfection today than you were yesterday, and if you are committed to being closer to perfection tomorrow and every day thereafter, you can become, and remain, a great leader. That is, if you do the other things that great leadership requires.

Conduct

Conduct generally refers to what you do and how you do it, and it is important to remember that your conduct flows from your character. A prime example is the story of a fox and a rattlesnake stuck on an island in the middle of a rising flood. Knowing that he would drown if he didn't do something quick, the snake asked the fox to let him ride on its back as the fox swam to safety. All was well until they reached the safety of high ground whereupon the snake bit the fox. The dying fox said, "Why did you bite me after I saved your life?" The snake replied, "You knew what I was when you picked me up!" Obviously, the character of the rattlesnake had not changed simply because of the good deed done by the fox.

True Leadership Principle: Conduct flows from character.

There are many actions a great leader takes– too many to cover in this one book – but there are a few critical ones that I will mention. First: listen. Great leaders are great listeners. They listen to everybody from the janitor to the CEO, and everyone in between. They listen to their customers, their suppliers, their competitors, their friends, neighbors, their family members, and even to leadership experts! They listen with the intent to learn and to understand, not to rebut an argument or to formulate a response. You must take listening seriously and in sequence – listen first to understand, ask clarifying questions. Then (and only then) when you understand as clearly and fully as possible in the present moment, think through and formulate your response. Most wars, literally and figuratively, can be avoided by this type of listening. It usually works if only one party is responding like this, and it always works when all parties are.

True Leadership Principle: Great leaders listen to understand, not to rebut or comment.

Another important aspect of conduct is consistency. A big part of your job as a leader is to paint the vision of where we are going and why we are going there, and then consistently keep that vision visible to yourself and everyone else. A great leader can sometimes resemble a broken record – saying and doing the same things over and over again.

A friend and mentor of mine told me many years ago to put my goals in concrete and my plans in sand. The goals and the vision should not waver. That consistency creates predictability, predictability builds trust, and trust is essential for great leadership to function. It is impossible to make people do and think things that they don't choose to do. Viktor Frankl learned that even in the most extreme circumstances people still have the freedom to choose how they think and behave. Since most will never be in a situation as horrific as a concentration camp, you can be certain that you will never be able to control the behavior of anyone but yourself. In fact, you should never even make the attempt because of the damage it does to trust and effectiveness. However, if you want to be a great leader, you must always control the mindset and behavior of one person– yourself. Consistently controlling yourself, and consistently developing your own character, conduct, and charisma will make you a predictable, yet effective, leader that people will trust and follow of their own free will. The ones who do not choose to follow you will leave, and the ones you need will tend to be automatically attracted to your team. It's almost unbelievable what happens when you're consistent.

The trick is to do all this without becoming inflexible, which is why great leaders listen to everyone. They are always learning, and applying what they have learned. Great leaders train themselves to have an insatiable curiosity about everything. And, since no one is perfect, great leaders also focus on what they do best, and hire the rest. They capture and use ideas from everywhere. Steve Jobs had to learn this lesson the hard way, as do most of us. When he tried to micromanage, he got fired from his own company. Later, when he came back as a much wiser and more flexible leader, he incorporated ideas from art, design, ergonomics, and social trends to create the products that propelled Apple from a computer company, to a premier company that is viewed today as much more than that.

True Leadership Principle: Great leaders are consistent and predictable (but not inflexible, boring, or overbearing).

True Leadership Principle: Great leaders focus on what they do best and hire the rest.

Charisma

Charisma is the third of the three "C's" and is the most visible of the three. It's all about effective communication which, thankfully, anyone can develop and improve. While some people are more naturally talented at this, almost everyone can develop it to a significant degree if they are willing to put in the work. Again, this is a lifestyle choice and must be worked on every day. Great leaders, like great athletes, must be humble and teachable and need continual coaching to reach and maintain their potential. Once you let your pride allow you to think you have arrived, you are actually on your way down.

True Leadership Principle: Great leaders are humble. Humble means teachable.

Charisma is essential for a number of reasons, the most important being the power of the first impression. In general, you have between seven and thirty seconds to make a good first impression, and if you do it poorly, statistically forty percent of people will write you off. Once that happens it is almost impossible to get them to believe in your vision. While it is possible to eventually gain credibility after making a poor first impression, it is a long and hard road. I know this little fact does not seem fair, and I agree that it really isn't, but fair or not, it is reality.

The trick is to remember that the whole process is backwards. Most people tend to work on their charisma first, neglecting character and conduct. While it can appear that charisma is the most important of the three "C's" because it is the most visible, followed by conduct (which is also visible), and character (which is not directly visible), the reality is just the opposite. For long-term success and greatness as a leader, character comes first, conduct comes in second, and charisma is in third place in terms of importance. Worse yet, charisma is the easiest to develop while character (the most important) is the most difficult. Failure to realize this is what makes it possible to create a Hitler or the many other charismatic, character deficient, "so called" leaders that litter the pages of history and the evening news. Sadly, they appear to flourish for a while, which makes the eventual unraveling failure that much worse, and their fall affects many more people than it should. Yoda was right, young Padawan, the quick and easy path does lead to the dark side!

Despite the danger, charisma is essential for effective leadership, and the risk is worth the reward. After all…

True Leadership Principle: Nothing good can ever be accomplished without some risk.

I like to break charisma down into two parts – basic communication (the words we use in speaking and writing) and presence (or non-verbal communication). Obviously, I am using basic communication (a.k.a. words) in writing this book. The advantage of written communication is that it leaves a record that can be referred to again. You can read and re-read this book if you want to, and I would highly recommend that you do. I find that I learn something new every time I re-read something. This happens because each time I read it, my experience and development level are different (hopefully in a good way) and because I am focusing on different problems and concerns, so my selective perception kicks in and allows me to see something that I missed each time I read it before. You want to hear something crazy? That even happens when I re-read my own books! How's that for goofiness? I find myself asking, "How could I have possibly known that when I wrote it?" The answer is that I probably didn't (at least consciously) but such is the power of time, experience, and selective perception. The new messages were imbedded there the whole time, without me even knowing it consciously. Maybe my subconscious mind knew, but my conscious mind certainly didn't!

Here's the problem: when you are limited to just using communication with words, whether written like this, read out loud, or spoken, you are severely restricted. Words only contain seven percent of the information. The other ninety-three percent of potential information is contained in your non-verbal presence. These are things like tone, pitch, pacing, the volume of your speech, your movements, posture, positioning, stance, eye contact, and so on. Essentially, your body language. I find this very frustrating when I write since, as a professional speaker, I do best in person where I can communicate with both my words and with my presence.

In fact, if you really want get the full message, you should contact me and bring me in to speak to you or your group. That way you can get the full one hundred percent, instead of just seven! Some people can get everything they need from a book, but most require the full experience to really be able to retain and apply the message.

True Leadership Principle: Charisma is 7% verbal communication and 93% presence. To be effective, a great

leader must develop and use both their charisma and their presence.

This brings up another point. If you want to become a great leader, you must practice using your charisma to communicate with people face-to-face. Great leaders continually practice and improve their charisma one-on-one and in large and small groups. How else can they effectively cast their vision and enroll (and re-enroll) people, including themselves, in that vision? Great leaders do this even if they don't particularly like talking to people—especially to groups—because they know they must do this in order to be effective and successful. There is no better way to influence people than by speaking to them face-to-face.

Now, I recognize that the number-one fear listed in every poll is the fear of speaking in public. Fear of death usually follows at number two, which means that most people would rather be in the box than preaching the eulogy! However, great leaders do it anyway, because they know it is necessary. After all, one of the most important character traits of great leaders is courage – especially social courage. By social courage, I mean the ability to face the risk of failing in public, and even the possibility of being subjected to public ridicule, shame, and even hostility because you know that what you are doing is right and needed.

True Leadership Principle: Courage, especially social courage, is an essential part of a leaders' charisma.

The biggest problem with charisma is that when you have it, people tend to think you are a leader, even if you have a serious flaw in your character or conduct. Sadly, most people who fall into this trap actually start to believe that they are great leaders, when in fact, they could use a few pointers. Charisma is so powerful, and first impressions are so significant that it's very easy for people to be fooled (and to fool themselves) into thinking that their charisma is all that's required to be a leader. Nothing could be further from the truth, and that's why those "so-called" leaders always fail in the long term. Their foolishness, arrogance, ego-centrism, pride, and lack of wisdom doom them from the start. Far too often that failure is spectacular and catastrophic to the point that organizations fail and vanish, fortunes and livelihoods are lost, and sometimes people even die as a result.

I hope you can see from all this that the idea of a "born leader" is a total myth. People are not born as leaders; they're born as babies! While some people are born with more talent for leadership than most, just like some people are born with more athletic, or artistic, or whatever talent than most, no one is a born leader. Every leader must develop their leadership in the same way – continuously, constantly, and over a lifetime of experience. Of course, this means that you too can develop yourself into a great leader, if you are willing to pay the price and do the necessary work. It all boils down to you– your priority and your commitment. If you make that development into a priority and keep that commitment to develop yourself, your leadership skills will increase a little bit every day. Just remember to keep growing.

So, there you have it – the three "Cs" of great leadership. You may be wondering how I know this stuff, so I'll share a little bit of my story, and hopefully you can relate and will learn some things that will help you on your journey to great leadership. First of all, I always tell people that wisdom helps you make good decisions, and wisdom is only gained by making bad decisions! That's a clue of how I learned what I have. I have become a better leader, only by starting out as a bad one. I've made a lot of mistakes, but I've learned from them. Although, I occasionally had to make the same mistake more than once to learn my lesson. But what can I say? Nobody's perfect.

True Leadership Principle: Wisdom helps you make good decisions and wisdom is gained by making bad decisions!

Once I got into a taxi in New York City and asked the cab driver, "How do I get to Carnegie Hall?" He turned around and said, "Practice! Practice! Practice!"

Now, here's the thing about that story. A lot of people have heard that practice makes perfect, but that's not true. Practice makes permanent. You can practice a bad golf swing and groove it to the point that you could do it in your sleep, but all you will end up with is a permanent bad golf swing. The truth is perfect practice makes perfect permanent. That's the real key.

True Leadership Principle: Perfect practice makes perfect permanent.

For over 3 decades I have made my living as a professional speaker, author, and leader. I have somewhere north of thirty thousand hours speaking in front of people professionally, from groups as small as one to groups of thousands. Now here's the thing, it is possible to have the same one

hour of experience thirty thousand times, but thankfully that isn't the case here. I should think I would be very bored with it all by now if it were! When I started out, I was actually really bad at it! After all, I was an electrical engineer with an MBA, and you do know the difference between an introverted engineer and an extroverted engineer, don't you? The extroverted engineer stares at your shoes instead of his! So I really had a long way to go to get where I am today.
One thing to remember is this:

True Leadership Principle: All leaders are speakers and all speakers are leaders.

When you are up in front, you are up in front, period! Your leadership, good or bad, is on display and you can't fake it or hide it—at least not for very long. What I want you to understand from this is that I have worked very hard, for decades, and I'm still learning, improving, and growing every day. For example, writing this book is a growing experience. It has forced me to think clearly enough to be able to communicate well, despite only having seven percent of my charisma available for the job. However, this does also have the side benefit of making me better at expressing these ideas face-to-face when I have the opportunity to do so.

I have also had to work very hard on improving my conduct. Have you ever seen how awkward most engineers are in social situations? If I hadn't worked on that, and weren't still working on it, how effective do you think I would have become? The answer is – not very. I've had to work the hardest on my character, of course, since every leader has to do that, and I am no exception.

I wasn't raised very well. I don't say this to blame anyone, because my parents did the best they knew how. Unfortunately, what they knew wasn't very good. I once had a professional counselor who had worked with people in the penal system for many years, who, after hearing my story said to me, "You are the only person I have ever met with a background like yours who has never been to prison. Why is that?"

As you can imagine, I was completely surprised by that question and didn't have an immediate answer. But, as I have thought about it, I have found that the answer is that I somehow had within me a burning desire to improve, learn, and grow and a belief that I could do so. I personally believe that God put it there. Despite the difficulties, mistakes, the failures along the way, I still felt that passion. No matter how bleak things sometimes looked (I was homeless for a time, and I've had cancer and a number of other things I've had to deal with), I have never lost that desire, and still perform from that place today. I think that's been the biggest key for me, and it may even be the key for you too. That desire has kept me moving forward, has fueled my thirst to learn, study, practice, find mentors, and all the other things that I have done and continue to do. I keep improving and moving forward, so I become better and better at who I am and what I do.

True Leadership Principle: Great leaders have a burning desire to move forward, and an absolute belief that they can always find a way to do so.

The Framers

Why are the "Framers" the "Framers" and how does framing help me?

What to learn:
Why are the Founders referred to as "The Framers"?
Why is framing crucial?
Who sets the frames and how and why must they do that?
Why is proper framing essential to your success as a leader?

What to avoid:
The framing form without the character-based substance.

In 1976, I was a student in electrical engineering at the University of Washington carrying 18 upper-division credits, married with 4 young children, and working two 20 hour per week jobs. Since I wasn't busy enough, I decided I needed to build a house. I had worked on several other residential construction projects before so I wasn't a complete rookie, the law allowed me to be the contractor on my own home, and I did have an experienced mentor to help me, so away I went.

If you've ever built a house, or seen one built, you know that for what seems like a very long time there doesn't appear to be much happening besides a hole in the ground. Then, the foundation finally gets poured. And then for a while longer it looks like a hole in the ground with some concrete in it. Then the framing begins, and in just a few days it suddenly looks like a house. Once the framing is finished the house can be closed and locked. Then again quite a long time passes where there is not much visible progress (at least from the outside), until the house is finally finished and ready for someone to move in. The point here is that the frame really defines the house. It not only makes the house look like a house, but everything after the framing is complete depends upon that frame.

The interesting parallel here is that the original copies of the Constitution that were sent to the various states for ratification were not titled, "The Constitution of the United States of America" like the document is today. They were simply titled, "A Frame of Government" which is one reason why the people who created the Constitution are often referred to as "The Framers." Just like building a house, constructing a government also depends on how you frame it.

That being said, how does the idea of a frame best apply to the leadership principles embedded in the Constitution? Oren Klaff once said that frames are the mental structures that outline our worldview and put our relationships into the context of that worldview. The frame you construct around a situation completely controls its meaning by simplifying the complexities and creating a clear way of interpreting that situation and the relationships related to it.

Think about this. In the case of the Constitution, the Framers defined the mental structures (which then became the structures of the three branches of government, checks and balances, guarantees of the people's inherent rights, etc.) that defined the relationships not only between the three branches of government, but also between the Federal government and the States, and ultimately, between the Federal Government and the actual sovereign power, "We the People." Proper framing keeps the focus on what is most important—human relationships – and the Framers clearly kept that in mind when they created the document.

True Leadership Principle: Framing is one of the most crucial leadership principles every leader must get good at and practice constantly.

Preambles and mission statements are full of framing. One of the best examples of this is a document that many of these same Framers created and signed a few years earlier than the Constitution was created, The Declaration of Independence. The Framers were operating from the same principles contained in the Declaration when they later developed the Constitution. A few of those framing statements are: "We hold these truths to be self-evident, that all men are created equal, that they are endowed by their Creator with certain unalienable Rights, that among these are Life, Liberty and the pursuit of Happiness. - That to secure these rights, Governments are instituted among

Men, deriving their just powers from the consent of the governed…"

They believed that human rights came from God, not from the government. Whether you believe in God or not, they did, and that was one of the most powerful frames that they established. Whether someone is more comfortable saying that rights are inherent in the human condition, or bestowed upon us by the universe or universal energy, or whatever they believe in, what is important is that we agree that they pre-exist and supersede government, just as the Framers believed.

Another powerful ideal that they established was this– all people are created equal. This is clearly untrue if you believe equal means identical, because no two people are identical – even identical twins. Some people are shorter, some are taller, some are more talented in one area, some in another and so on. What they meant is that all people should be treated as equals by their government. In other words, they rejected the idea of royalty and royal birthrights, and that some people are inherently better simply because of who their parents are.

The last, and most powerful, frame I want to point out is that they believed that the purpose of government is to secure and protect these unalienable and inherent rights of the people. These frames are among the frames that underlie and support the Constitution, and are powerful leadership principles that we can still learn from today.

These are the lessons that we need to learn from these frames, if we want to be great leaders. As leaders, we need to recognize, include, and operate from them. As a leader, it is crucial that I treat people fairly and respectfully, and never attempt to violate their basic, inherent, God-given rights. Any time that I do so, I will instantly lose respect, credibility, and trust, and without these things I cannot be a great leader. In fact, I probably lose any ability I initially had to lead effectively, much less greatly. These true leadership principles are independent of anyone's religious beliefs, as they exist within us as humans, and potential leaders. We must recognize that whatever organization we lead – business, governmental, a family, etc. – that organization exists, in part, to protect the inherent rights of its members. In short, every organization has at least two purposes: the obvious one, such as making a profit, providing services, etc., AND protecting the inherent rights of its members.

True Leadership Principle: All great leaders treat people fairly and respectfully. They never attempt to violate any person's inherent rights. If a leader violates this, they will lose trust and never be able to lead effectively.

So how does that apply to us as leaders, especially if we want to become great leaders? We must accept the responsibility to set the frames. This is a combination of communicating the vision and setting an example by the way we behave. We must both "talk the talk" AND "walk the walk" to be trusted and credible. After all, whoever controls the vocabulary controls the discussion. If I'm the leader, then it's my responsibility to see that everyone is on the same page, and the best way to do that is by being the best and most charismatic communicator I can possibly be. Part of that is defining the terms and the parameters of the discussion. This discussion will eventually create an agreement throughout the organization on why we are doing what we are doing, where we are going, and how we intend to get there. At the very least, it is my responsibility to ensure that everyone is clear on the first, and each consecutive, step that we are going to take so that we can move forward.

Ideally, I create a consensus by painting mental pictures of the vision. Always verbally, and often by actually drawing and sharing simple diagrams and pictures. I then must enroll first myself, then others in that vision. After all, I can't effectively sell what I don't absolutely believe in myself, so I must first decide whether or not I am confidently enrolled. Actually, this is something that I do every day, sometimes many times a day, in order to stay focused and on task. It's one of the necessary disciplines every leader must learn, and actively practice daily for the rest of their lives if they want to be a great leader – self-enrollment.

True Leadership Principle: You must enroll yourself first, and keep yourself enrolled, before you can effectively enroll others and keep them enrolled.

Until you as a leader can lead yourself effectively, you can never lead others effectively. However, as you get better and better at leading yourself effectively, you will also get better and better at leading others effectively. Self-leadership is an absolutely necessary skill that all great leaders possess and continue to develop and improve on a daily basis.

True Leadership Principle: Self-leadership is the first skill you must develop, practice, constantly improve, and maintain if you want to be a great leader.

Remember, the decision to become a great leader is a lifestyle choice. It defines much of what you do every day and, gradually and almost imperceptibly, what and who you become in the long run as both a leader and as a human being.

True Leadership Principle: Seeing the vision yourself is useless unless and until you can successfully communicate it to others and enroll them in that vision.

The next step in framing is to enroll others in your vision. No one ever accomplished anything big, hairy, and audacious by themselves. It can't be done alone. Self- leadership is the required first step, but it is only the *first* step.

The key here is to become a charismatic communicator. Without that skill you will always have a difficult time attracting and keeping the people and resources you will need in order to accomplish your vision. In order to make that happen and enroll others, you must first learn to listen to them and find out what their goals and dreams are. This is the first step in the process of establishing and maintaining trusting relationships with all the people you interact and work with. Most importantly, you must apply this step to yourself (if you don't trust yourself you are in deep trouble), and to all those you interact with in your life – at home, at work, vendors, suppliers, customers, clients, employees, co-workers, peers – basically, with everyone you meet. Once you begin to develop trusting relationships, people will start revealing their real, often hidden, desires, goals, and motivations both personally and professionally. Just as important (maybe even more important) they will begin to reveal their priorities. This is where enrollment happens – when you can help someone understand how your vision aligns with their own personal goals and priorities.

More often than not, they aren't very clear themselves on their goals and priorities, so it becomes your job as the leader to help them figure things out. Once there is clarity on their goals it becomes possible to help them move into the emotional state of enrolling them into your vision. Then it becomes possible to help them commit, or "buy in" to the vision you are presenting. Remember, we, as human beings, are emotional creatures and make ALL decisions based upon emotion. Significant decisions are never made logically – NEVER! What we actually do is make an emotional decision, and then create a logical sounding rationalization (at least, it sounds logical to us) to justify the emotional decision we have made. This way, we can feel less anxiety about our decisions and maintain the self-illusion that we are logical creatures. What others choose to do is their concern, but if I want to be a great leader I have discovered that I must be as brutally honest with myself as I possibly can, and part of that is recognizing I am an emotional being. Actually, the more important the decision, the more that is at stake, the more emotional my decision processes become. That's true for me, and most likely true for you, whether you like it or believe it or not – just like gravity!

True Leadership Principle: All decisions are emotionally based. That's just how humans work!

True Leadership Principle: Charismatic communication is an absolutely essential leadership skill that must be constantly practiced, used, and improved every day of your life if you want to be an effective, and possibly even a great, leader.

The Real Leaders

❦

Who are the real leaders?

What to learn:
What's the most valuable skill set?
Why is that the case?
Why does this matter to me?
What do I do about it?

What to avoid:
Thinking it applies to someone else and not you.

A couple years ago, I received that dreaded letter that instructed me to appear for jury duty. I've received similar letters before and they are always at inconvenient times. While it is sometimes possible to be excused from jury duty, I had no such luck, so I showed up as instructed. I wasn't too worried because I had never been selected before and expected that would be the case again. Unfortunately, I was wrong and was selected to sit on the jury for a criminal domestic aggravated assault case, a second-degree felony.

I was surprised that they selected me given my background as a leadership expert, bestselling author on leadership, experienced actor, and professional speaker. Maybe the defense attorney was out of challenges. Maybe he was naïve, or he thought he could convince me of his client's innocence, and if he did then I would be able to convince the jury to produce a not guilty verdict. If so, he was probably right about that. I don't know, but had I been him I would have never seated someone like me. Nevertheless, there I was, sitting in a courtroom for two very long days.

The first thing I did was make a couple of decisions. First, since I was stuck there I decided I was going to be elected jury foreman. After all, if you're not the lead dog the view never changes. The second decision I made was that I was going to do my best to ensure that the accused received a fair trial, and that the other jurors would be able to have their full say on the verdict.

I then proceeded to endure two days of some of the worst presentations I have ever been subjected to. Both attorneys were dismal in their presentation skills! It was all I could do to focus on the evidence which was clearly in the prosecution's favor – including bloody pictures of the assault. The only bright spot in the whole ordeal was the expert witness testimony of the doctor who had to repair the damage. His presentation was actually quite good, and included both before and after pictures. I actually learned a lot about reconstructive plastic surgery.

When they finally sent us off to deliberate, the first thing we did was elect a jury foreman: me. That took about two minutes since I had been subtly working the group for the last two days without them even noticing (or at least not caring if they did notice) using the character, conduct, and charisma elements that were introduced earlier. Then we spent over three hours working our way to the guilty verdict, making sure that everyone was in full agreement, again using those same three elements.

The point of this story is that leadership skills matter – they matter a lot! In fact, leadership skills are the most valuable skills that exist. As a predictor of success it has been shown that emotional quotient (EQ) is as much as a 27:1 point-for-point better predictor of success than IQ. In other words, a one-point increase in EQ is equivalent to a 27-point increase in IQ as a success predictor. That's amazing, but I believe that if anyone could ever figure out how to measure leadership quotient (LQ) that would be at least 27:1 over EQ! I don't think they are likely to ever be able to measure LQ effectively, but leadership skills are clearly the rarest and most highly leveraged of all the skill sets. Getting back to our story, the question is, "Who are the real leaders in this situation?" The answer is that we, the jury in this case, were the real leaders. While I was elected to be the foreman and spokesman for the group, all the jurors collectively were the real leaders.

True Leadership Principle: Leadership skills are the most powerful of all the skill sets.

We, the jury, found out after our verdict that the defendant was a very dangerous person. He was a multiple long-time offender, who was shackled during the whole trial beneath the table out of our view and never allowed to stand in our presence so that we could not see his chains. Despite the best efforts of the judge and both attorneys to keep certain facts from us, and their unwillingness to share with us certain information that we requested, we were still able to reach the correct decision due to both the genius of the jury system and the leadership principles we exercised. We were clearly the leaders, and everyone else in the courtroom had to abide by our decisions. While the judge and the attorneys are officers of the court and essentially representing the government, we, the jury, represented "We the People" and we were the ones with the power, and the responsibility, to determine guilt or innocence. This tension between the government and its representatives and "We the People" is a necessary and very powerful component of great leadership, and applies in every leadership situation.

So how does this apply to "We the People" and how does it apply to us as leaders in our various roles and organizations? The thing to remember is that everyone is a leader at some time and at some level. Some of us as very aware of that, while some are not, but it's still the truth. Wouldn't it be in the best interest of the people around us if we improved our leadership skills? After all, great leadership is one of the most important, yet lacking, elements in our world. It's missing, yet needed, just about everywhere you look. If you want to set yourself apart from the crowd, if you want to make a greater impact on the world, or if you simply want to make your life better, just start developing better leadership skills. I mean, think about it. If you could increase your own LQ by just one point, that would have the same impact on you and those around you as increasing your IQ by 729 points! (That's 27 times 27 if you do the math.) The impact of improving your leadership skills is huge! Just imagine what will happen if you increase your leadership by 2 points, or 3, or even more! That is how you can really change the world! That's how we all can.

True Leadership Principle: Everyone is a leader at some point so developing leadership skills is important to, and helps, everyone.

So how do you develop and increase your leadership skills? Great question, and I'll get back to that, but first…

THE QUESTION

&

What are their incentives?

What to learn:
Short term vs. long term thinking
Band-Aids vs. real healing
Identifying the real incentives
The simple answer - aligning incentives

What to avoid:
Thinking that simple fixes are quick and easy to implement

A number of years ago I was the Legislative District Chairman for my political party. This meant that I had certain meetings I had to attend, and certain responsibilities I had to care for. This was especially true as the time for the caucuses approached as I was responsible for seeing that all the precinct chair people had their materials, and knew how to run their caucus. The busiest time for me started just before the caucuses, through the nominating conventions and the primaries, and culminating with the general election. It was an interesting process, and I personally knew many of the elected officials as a result. But that wasn't the most interesting, or valuable, lesson I learned.

I learned that any involved person has an inordinate amount of influence on legislation, and even on the development of regulations to implement that legislation. And the reason is frighteningly simple – almost no one who is not a full-time lobbyist ever takes the time to meet with their elected officials and give their input! It's no wonder politicians seem out of touch with most of their constituency, because they actually are out of touch with them! Once I understood this, I was able to accomplish some very interesting things.

When our state legislator moved out of the district, I was one of three people who were interviewed by the governor to replace him. The governor chose one of the other two but it was still a very enlightening experience, and I learned a lot about politicians from it. On another occasion, I was able to influence child support legislation to include the needs of fathers and not just the needs of mothers into the equation. I was also able to influence IRS regulations on business mileage deductions by taking a short trip to Washington, DC to meet with congressmen, senators, and IRS officials. In fact, on that trip I was sitting with Senator Jake Garn on the couch in his office as we both listened to Senator Bob Dole read a commendation to Senator Garn into the Congressional Record regarding him being the first

"Senator in Space" prior to his space shuttle mission. This was especially exciting for me since I had actually designed part of the space shuttle system when I was working as an engineer for Boeing Aerospace.

There's a fundamental problem with politics that is also shared with the business world, and it's deadly to great leadership. That problem is short-term thinking. In the political process it shows up because the incentive for politicians is to get re-elected and, depending on the office they hold that is only two, four, or six years away. In reality, it's actually a pretty short window (the older I get the shorter 2, 4, or 6 years seems to be) and that leads to short-term thinking and short-term actions. The same is true with business where the short-term focus from investors is based upon the next quarter's performance and dividends or, at most, performance over the next year. Since great leadership is focused on the long-term, there is little incentive for great leadership in those arenas unless a person is really character driven. In that case the incentive and motivation to be a great leader comes from within (which is the only place it can ever really come from anyway).

The problem this creates in both politics and business is that the "so-called" leaders tend to fold under the pressure of short-term thinking. Then instead of fixing the serious structural problems, which takes a long time and often is very painful, they just put "Band-Aids" on the problems to ease the immediate pain. The problem is, of course, that the underlying serious issues don't get addressed, and the organization gets sicker and sicker over time. Sadly, in the political case, they keep getting re-elected, and in the business case, they keep getting their annual bonuses – at least for the time being. At some point, the situation will become so bad that the serious problems have to be fixed, or the organization will fail. Unfortunately, by then the structural problems are so much worse that it requires major painful surgery to fix them, not just a Band-Aid.

The answer to this problem is actually pretty simple: just change everyone's incentives and align them with long-term goals and thinking. While it is simple to say and understand, it is not easy to do. Long-term thinking is a higher-level leadership skill. It is based in character and wisdom, and it can be very difficult to influence people to buy into that. As it turns out, that in itself (aligning incentives with long-term goals and visions) is a long-term leadership challenge. It's difficult to do, but really is worth it because it is necessary for the long-term health and success of organizations.

True Leadership Principle: Great leaders are constantly working to align people's incentives with the long-term goals and vision.

Section II: The Leadership Gap

THE LEADERSHIP GAP: PART I

ॐ

Why are most politicians such lousy leaders and what does that teach me?

What to learn:
What are we missing here?
Incentive issues
Character issues
How does this help us in our own organizations and lives?

What to avoid:
Knee-jerk, emotional, quick fixes

Although politicians are certainly members of "We the People," their incentives and interests are not the same as ours in most cases. That's why, too often, it really is a situation of Us vs. Them or Politicians vs. "We the People". I want to make a clarification here. First of all, I'm not suggesting that all politicians are bad people, because I certainly do not believe that.

There are those who hold political office who are true statesmen, not politicians, and there is a huge difference. As Linda Lingle said, "Politicians all too often think about the next election. Statesmen think about the next generation." This is the real difference between politicians and statesmen – short-term vs. long-term thinking, planning, and action. In fact, that's also one of the major differences between management and leadership. Management tends to have a relatively short-term focus while leadership is mostly focused long-term. It would be really great for all of us if those holding elected office were all statesmen, but sadly that is not the case.

Another issue is that, far too often, character (the #1 trait of a great leader) is lacking in many politicians. All you have to do is read or see the news, and you'll see this problem paraded before your eyes almost every day. For most politicians, once elected, their biggest concern is usually getting re-elected. Even if they begin with the best of intentions, which many of them do, they quickly discover that the influence and money they need to get elected repeatedly require them to compromise their principles and agendas and "toe the party line" in order to get the funds and other resources they need to stay in office. Compromise is important and necessary in areas where it is appropriate, but it is disastrous in character issues. Great leaders never compromise their character because they understand that solid character is the foundation of their leadership. It is the thing that draws followers to them and makes their leadership legitimate. These incentives for politicians are rarely long-term as they are only focused on the next election. By definition they rarely foster good leadership practices, since good leadership is almost always focused on the long-term results of what we do today. Short-term things need to be considered, but the leadership focus is always long-term.

True Leadership Principle: Solid character is the foundation that makes leadership legitimate.

Great leaders don't care who gets the credit and, in fact, usually spread the credit around to all the people involved in a success. When was the last time you saw a politician do that? One important characteristic of great leaders is that they truly care about the welfare and the success of those they are leading. Not just lip service to garner votes, but true caring. Great leaders will sacrifice anything necessary to attain a worthy goal – including themselves and their careers if necessary. They are not selfish. Again, not a behavior often seen in politicians.

So what do we, as leaders, need to learn from this? Firstly, that the quick-fix, knee-jerk type solutions rarely work long-term (unless you happen to be very lucky every once in a while). These types of solutions must be avoided. The examples of this type of action that we see from politicians are not a good model for success, and should not be followed by those who intend to be successful. Secondly, we need to establish that the incentives of our organizations are the correct ones for the long-term success that we desire. We need to advocate and work to the degree possible to help our politicians by helping change their incentives as well, wherever and whenever we can.

True Leadership Principle: Quick-fix, "knee-jerk" solutions rarely work long-term and are poor leadership practice.

The Leadership Gap:
Part II

❧

Why are most executives such lousy leaders and what does that teach me?

What to learn:
The differences between good management and good leadership
Incentive issues, ego issues, and character flaws
Great leaders listen to different advice
Great leaders stay on track despite opposition

What to avoid:
Forgetting who the real boss is and who we serve

The biggest problem most executives have is that they think they are leaders when, in fact, they are just managers. Too often they really don't know the difference between leadership and management. You see, management is like other technical skills – it can be trained. Leadership, on the other hand, cannot be trained, but must be developed. The training process and the development process are diametrically opposed, which is why so many great managers are not successful in making the transition to becoming a great (or even an average) leader. The fact remains that businesses have to be managed and people have to be led, but when an executive tries to manage people with the same types of processes as they manage things like money, time, projects, and other resources, they are destined to fail. Great leadership is infinitely more complicated than great management, as the skills must be continually honed and practiced. You can never really "arrive" at great leadership in the same way that you can become a great manager. The decision to become a great leader requires the choice to adopt a lifestyle of continual improvement, growth, change, failure, discomfort, and always stretching the boundaries of "the box". It is a decision that will change you– not a decision to change "them."

Another problem, like in the case of politicians, is incentives. If an executive gets bonuses based upon monthly, quarterly, or even annual results their incentives are inherently short term as opposed to long term. As I mentioned earlier, leadership must have a long term focus. Management tends to have a much shorter focus than leadership because most management decisions are based on timeframes shorter than a year or two. Also, management is usually based upon metrics that are relatively easy to calculate. Managers will then compare actual performance to these numbers and work to get closer to those optimal results. There are a couple of problems with this. That approach can work but it is often difficult to determine which numbers are the most important.

If that decision is wrong (which it often is) it messes with the incentives for people, the issue of improper incentives being a matter that we have already discussed. The other problem is that many of the most important things cannot be easily measured or reduced to a metric. Because of this, management tends to ignore things like employee engagement and buy-in because they can't really be measured. Attempts to do so with surveys and such sometimes work well in very high trust environments, but if the organization is being managed too much and led too little, trust will be low so people will lie on their surveys for fear of repercussions.

Again, great leaders do not care who gets the credit, and wise leaders spread the credit around. This type of unselfishness is far too rare among those striving to "climb the corporate ladder." Another issue is that too many "so-called" leaders are so ego driven, so sure that they are right, or believe that they know more than they really do, so much so that they will not listen to others for insight or advice. They typically don't listen to outsiders and consultants and many don't even listen to their own people because they feel they must somehow remain separate and above those whose positions are lower on the organizational chart.

True Leadership Principle: Great leaders do not care who gets the credit and wise leaders spread the credit around.

Often, as with politicians, there is also a character issue with many executives, and they will bend and compromise where those with better character will stand their ground. The need to look good instead just being good is too strong of a temptation for too many. That always is bad for the long-term health of the organization and too often leads to poor performance, company loss, and even sometimes to prison. Great leaders will stay on track and hold true to their vision and goals despite pressure from the short-sighted – people like stock brokers, institutional investors, the media, directors, senior managers, and others who are only interested in this quarter's performance and dividend.

True Leadership Principle: Great leaders know it's better to be good than to look good.

THE LEADERSHIP GAP: PART III

꩜

Why are most of "We the People" such lousy leaders and how can I lead from anywhere in the organization?

What to learn:
You must learn to lead yourself before you can effectively lead others
Responsibility is a gift
Being responsible is your gift to others
You're never beaten until you quit

What to avoid:
Laziness, resignation, helplessness, victimhood, and entitlement mentality

Because of the leadership principles embodied in the Constitution, "We the People" are the ultimate governmental power. We are sovereign. The problem with that concept is that most of us don't understand what it means. Yes, we have freedoms – inherent in our humanity and specifically guaranteed by the Constitution and the Bill of Rights (the first ten amendments), but along with all freedoms there is the required flip side. We also have the responsibilities that are inseparably attached to those freedoms and here is where most of us, most of the time (and all of us some of the time, nobody's perfect) abdicate our sovereignty by shirking our responsibilities.

I've heard it said that there are three types of people – Sheep, Wolves, and Sheep Dogs. Most people are sheep – fat, dumb, happy, and just interested in finding the next blade of grass (or whatever) to satisfy their immediate needs. They don't plan or think too much and just kind of wander around or go where they are pushed or led – usually complaining loudly but not doing much else about it. Far too many of "We the People" fall into this category. We are not willing to do the required work to develop ourselves so that we can have something with which to help others. We follow human nature instead of fighting against that nature to develop ourselves for a bigger purpose. We abdicate our sovereignty.

Then there are the wolves.

The wolves are selfish and merciless. They are only interested in their own needs and wants, and will readily exploit the sheep, and even kill and eat them, if it gets them where they want to go. They are lacking in character and their conduct is unconscionable. They can also be very subtle and devious and appear to want to be good and helpful while they set their traps (remember the story of the wolf in sheep's clothing?). Left to themselves they will create disaster because they will first exploit and kill all of the sheep and then, due to their own shortsightedness, starve to death themselves because there is nothing left for them to eat. Unchecked, they will create total devastation. Sadly, too many politicians, executives, and other "so-called" leaders fall into this category. They only care about themselves and will do whatever they can get away with to get what they want – legality, morality, and ethics be damned.

Finally, there are the sheep dogs. The sheep dogs will do anything to protect the sheep from the wolves. They will go without sleep. They will risk injury, even death, fighting the wolves, all to protect the sheep. They lead the sheep to the best grass and the best water. The fascinating thing is that the ancestors of sheep dogs were wolves! Therefore, sheep dogs can fight just as well and hard as the wolves, when necessary, and defeat them because they have that fighting spirit still in their DNA. In fact, they can fight harder than the wolves because they are defending something much bigger than their own self-interest. Luckily, there are still a few sheep dogs among politicians, executives, and "We the People". The question is, "Why aren't we all (that is "We the People") working to become better sheep dogs?" That's our calling and our Constitutional duty as Americans - to be the sheep dogs. Why do you think our Constitution is the model for all other constitutions? Why do you think we have millions of people trying to come to America, instead of millions trying to leave?

That's why the Framers were inspired to create a Constitution based upon true leadership principles – principles that would stand the test of time if we utilize them in our personal lives, our families, our jobs and businesses, our government, and our other institutions.

The core true principle of leadership is self-leadership, which is based upon free will. "We the People" is really a statement and acknowledgement that all leadership begins with self-leadership. Until you can successfully lead yourself you cannot successfully lead others. As you become better at leading yourself, you naturally become better at leading others. This is why character is always number one, and the first step. Our second president, John Adams, said it this way, "Our Constitution was made only for a moral and religious people. It is wholly inadequate to the government of any other." And he was right. Even then, the first requirement for great leadership was good character, and that rings true, even still, today.

True Leadership Principle: If you can't lead yourself, you can't lead others effectively, but as you learn to lead yourself more effectively, you will be able to lead others more effectively.

A big part of great character is searching out and accepting responsibility. Great leaders are always responsible for something, that's really part of the definition of great leadership. But not only are they willing to accept responsibility for the outcome, but they actually seek it out and relish the opportunity to be responsible for it. For example, when the game was on the line, Michael Jordan always wanted the ball. Of course, if you are responsible for the outcome you also have the most impact on that outcome, and the outcome carries the mark of your leadership. The gift of leadership is the gift of responsibility, and the gift of responsibility is the leader's gift to the world. Great leaders are the ones who step up and say, "I'll see that it gets done." Someone has to do it, or nothing will ever get done! Since what they are doing will have a positive impact on the world (at least on one small part of it) taking responsibility is the leader's gift to the world.

True Leadership Principle: Responsibility is a gift, and taking responsibility is the leader's gift to the world.

That's really the blessing and the opportunity that the Constitution gives "We the People."The opportunity and the freedom to take responsibility and to make the world a better place. We all have the freedom and the responsibility to be sheep dogs, and as we do that, the world becomes a better place for all of us. We all have the ability and the opportunity to lead if we choose to. That is perhaps the greatest freedom that the leadership principles of the Constitution provide for us. To quote Winston Churchill (who was half American by the way), "Never, never, never give up!" Of course it's challenging and difficult. If it were easy, everyone would do it. You are never truly beaten until you quit.

True Leadership Principle: Great leaders NEVER give up!

Part of the problem is that "We the People" are not educated in leadership. This is because almost none of those teaching us, and the "so-called" leaders in government, business, education, the media, and elsewhere understand it either. After all, you can't teach what you don't know, and you can't lead where you won't go. This lack of knowledge is one of the reasons why "We the People" do such a poor job of leading. Ronald Regan put it this way, "Freedom is never more than one generation away from extinction. We didn't pass it to our children in the bloodstream. It must be fought for, protected, and handed on for them to do the same." Along with this problem is the fact that most of us, as well as those who are trying to teach us, don't understand how critical having great leadership really is. This is because not only are the effects of great leadership difficult to measure, but they don't show up right away. Leadership is long-term; its effects only show up clearly after some time has passed. Because we are conditioned that all problems can be solved in thirty minutes (minus commercials), or that it's all about some pithy sound bite, we don't usually have the patience to stay the course and let the leadership effects shine through. Lastly, since we aren't educated in leadership and don't really understand it very well, and don't even see it modeled very often, we don't practice it because we don't know how. This lack of education, understanding, and practice leads to lousy leadership.

True Leadership Principle: Great leaders are great because they are constantly learning, gaining understanding, and practicing great leadership.

THE LEADERSHIP GAP:
PART IV

৵

Why is it important to address the "Leadership Gap"?

What to learn:
All leadership gaps lead to disaster
Disaster is avoided by closing the leadership gaps
Identification of leadership gaps is the first and most challenging task
It's always possible to fix the gap

What to avoid:
Hopelessness, impatience, and feeling powerless

When I was in the US Air Force, we had a saying – a little poem actually (in truth we had a lot of them – most of which are not repeatable in polite company - but this one is) that went like this:

When in worry,
When in doubt,
Run in circles,
Scream and shout!

Too often that is what far too many of us do. We make a lot of noise, and may even get our fifteen minutes of fame for the noise, but actually do little or nothing else. We do absolutely nothing of value, and certainly nothing that really changes anything or anyone for the better. We tend to let the noise, the attention, and the appearance of progress substitute for real progress. The more of this type of behavior we see, the more we can be certain that there is little or no real leadership being exercised – at least by those engaging in that behavior. We know there is no self-leadership happening, and no one is stepping up to be a real leader, to properly channel the wasted energy and the noise.

The real issue here is that we tend to behave like this when we are frustrated and don't know what else to do. I get it, I've often felt the same way. But I have learned enough about leadership to respond differently than that now, at least most of the time. As I've said, "Nobody's perfect!" and I certainly include myself in that imperfect crowd. Let me give you an example.

It's the mid '80s and I'm sitting at my desk in my home office (which is in the basement of my home) looking out the window at the back yard when the phone rings. I pick it up and it's the controller of the company of which I am CEO (that we have taken from 0 to $6 million in 18 months) and he says, "We just had a board meeting that you were not invited to and you are no longer the CEO. Goodbye." Then the phone goes dead. I'm stunned to say the least, and as I hang up the phone I say to myself, "So now what am I going to do?" As I listen to the patter of little feet upstairs (I had 8 children under 15 years old at this point) knowing that I will lose my home along with my livelihood since it is all on the line for the business. I figure that one phone call cost me at least $1 million.

After a couple weeks of throwing myself a pity party, exploring my legal options, etc., I determine it is best to cut my losses and move forward. So I begin to analyze what went wrong and what I can do to avoid it happening again. In other words, what can I learn from all of this? As I worked to answer this question, I discovered something very profound that totally changed my life and my direction. The company was a technical company with an electronic product. In fact, I have an electrical engineering degree and I personally designed the original prototype of our product, so I have the technical skills aspect of the business covered. I also have an executive MBA, so I have the management skills to cover that aspect of the business as well (remember, management skills can be trained). I determine that neither of those are where my problem exists. I determine that I am a lousy leader, and that is the cause of my problem. So I determine that my fix is that I need to become an expert in leadership. (Turns out the board never did figure out the problem and find a good leader to fix it, so the company went bankrupt a couple years later anyway.)

What I'm saying is that I was a living, breathing example of a leadership gap. Leadership gaps lead to disaster.

So what I'm suggesting here is that if we want our lives, our families, our businesses, our communities, and our nation to run better, then we each need to suck it up and take on the responsibility to develop first, our own self-leadership, and second, our leadership skills in every area of our lives – instead of doing the run in circles, scream and shout thing. Through this experience, I learned something very profound…

True Leadership Principle: All things rise and fall based on the quality of the leadership – you, your family, your business, and your nation.

So there I am – faced with the reality that my part of the problems in my business (and actually in all the other areas of my life as well) are caused by the fact that I'm a lousy leader. Along with that, I'm scrambling to keep my family afloat financially (and emotionally, spiritually, etc.). I find myself faced with a decision. I've already decided that I need to fix the gap between my current level of leadership and the leader I can and need to be, but now I have to decide, "How am I going to fix this gap?"

The first thing I did was to prepare spiritually, because I intuitively knew this would be a huge and permanently life-changing process. So I read scriptures, prayed, spent time alone outdoors in the mountains, meditated, counseled with my wife and others, and gathered the spiritual and emotional resources to make a change this huge - at least, it was huge for me. I'm not suggesting that you do exactly what I did, because you have to use whatever process works for you. But I will tell you that in order to make a change of this magnitude, you will need massive amounts of spiritual and emotional strength. It's required, so gather it however you can. I can only say that my process works for me; you'll need to find your own.

I then started reading everything I could find on leadership and put my readings into practice. One of the things I learned was the value of mentors. I found that I could really accelerate my process by hanging out with great leaders – reading their books, listening to their audios, going to their events, and spending time one-on-one with them. I found out that it is really true–you do, in fact, become the average of the five people you hang out with most. So be very careful which five you choose and make sure they are where you want to be, or at least ahead of you on the that path. The reality is that no one is the perfect leader (well, there was this one guy about 2000 years ago, but beyond that...) and you can never "arrive" at perfect leadership. It is a lifestyle choice to improve your leadership every single day, without exception.

The other thing I learned is that true leadership principles are timeless. They have always existed, always worked, and they still exist and work exactly the same way today. I learned that they can be found everywhere in both the past and the present, and that there is evidence of success where they are applied and evidence of failure where they are not. They are readily available to use and very easy to find if you know what to look for and where to look. For instance, the Constitution of the United States of America. After all, the leadership principles there have worked exceptionally well for more than two hundred years and have created the most prosperous, and the greatest force for good in a nation that the world has ever seen (all this despite the imperfections of the citizens of the United States and the mistakes they have made). So this Constitution, and the leadership principles it contains must be a perfect place to look if you want to learn to be a better leader.

True Leadership Principle: True leadership principles are timeless.

Section III:
The Fix

Step 1:
Learn the Principles

❧

The leadership principles of "The Constitution," they've worked for over 200 years - they must be doing something right!

What to learn:
The so called modern leadership principles are not modern at all – they are timeless.
The principles that worked in 1789 work just as well today.
What are these underlying principles?
How can these principles be used in modern leadership practices?

What to avoid:
Overlooking the simple and the obvious in favor of more complicated answers.

"The Constitution of the United States was made not merely for the generation that then existed, but for posterity- unlimited, undefined, endless, perpetual posterity."
—Henry Clay

The Preamble – the "Mission Statement"

There's a story of a bus driver going down the street pass- ing up bus stop after bus stop without even slowing down. Finally, one of the passengers leans up and asks the driver, "Where are we going?" The driver answers, "I have no idea but we are sure making great time!" That's what it's like to be part of an organization without a clear mission that ev- eryone in the organization buys into. Lots of activity but no direction and no discernable progress.

Every organization needs a mission statement. This allows us to determine who we are, what we're doing, and where we're going. It lays out the purpose and the scope of the organization at its more general and most basic level. As such the mission statement of the United States of America, a.k.a. The Preamble, reads as follows:

> **"We the People** of the United States, in Order to form a more perfect Union, establish Justice, insure domestic Tranquility, provide for the common de- fence, promote the general Welfare, and secure the Blessings of Liberty to ourselves and our Posterity, do ordain and establish this Constitution for the United States of America."

(Note: defence uses the British spelling as opposed to the later American spelling, defense)

Like every good mission statement, it lays out the purposes and the priorities of the organization that it defines (and in this case, actually creates). How can you ever lead an organization of people without knowing the purpose and the priorities? And why would anyone ever want to be part of an organization without knowing and agreeing with its purpose and priorities? This is basic leadership 101. There must be a clear vision and it must be agreed to by both the leaders and those being led.

True Leadership Principle: Every organization needs a Mission Statement to lay out the basic frames of the organization and its purpose. All involved people need to buy in to that Mission Statement.

The Articles – (a.k.a. "the frames")

Framing was discussed earlier and is one of the most important functions of great leadership. The seven articles of the Constitution provide the framework of the government of the United States by establishing the three branch structure and defining the relationships between those structures, the states, and the people of the United States. The Constitution does this by establishing the frames based upon true leadership principles. Let's take a look.

Article I

True Leadership Principle: People need to feel they have a voice and an impact on decisions – either directly, by someone who represents their interests and their point of view, or both.

In the case of Article I, which outlines the Legislative Branch of the government, the compromise that the Framers reached made sure that every voice would be heard. The smaller states wanted to guarantee that they would not be dominated by the states with more population and money, while many in the more populated states felt they should have a greater say. In order to address both concerns two groups were created – the Senate, where all states are equally represented, and the House, where the representation is based upon population. Both groups have to agree on all legislation, so both perspectives are represented.

True Leadership Principle: Compromise is often the best tactic and most desirable course of action. It often leads to better answers, tactics, and approaches due to the mastermind principle (essentially, two or more heads are better than one).

As a leader you cannot always afford to compromise if you want the best out of yourself, your people, and your organization. Some things are open to compromise, and some are not. Certain things, if compromised will destroy credibility and trust. Great leadership always requires trust as one of the basic elements.

True Leadership Principle: Not everything is open to compromise. For example, no matter how many legislators a state has, each legislator only gets one vote. Changing that item was never included in the compromise. In other words, they did not make "some pigs more equal than others," to paraphrase George Orwell.

Anything that destroys trust must be avoided like the plague if great leadership is to be built and maintained. For example, suppose you are at a restaurant with some of your people and the waiter brings you too much change. What do you do? Most of us would probably correct the problem because we have an audience, but what if you didn't? How would that affect your credibility, your people's trust in you, and morale? These are clearly problems, but the real question is what do you do if you are there, the same thing happens, but nobody you know is around? What would you do then? Do your correct the mistake, the same as before, or do you pocket the extra? What does that do to your credibility and trust? After all, you never know who is watching, but even if no one is, you will know what you did.

True Leadership Principle: Great leadership requires two-way trust. The leader must trust their people and the people being led must trust the leader.

Let's up the ante once more. Now imagine that the survival of your company (or your home) is on the line and you have to get a loan in order to survive. You don't really qualify, but if you "fudge the numbers" a little it appears that you do, and you will get the loan that you need. What do you do then? If you give in and "do the smart thing," what does that do to trust? Even if no one else knows, what does that do to your self-image when you know you can't be trusted? When you can't trust yourself what happens to your character, your conduct, your charisma, and your ability to lead effectively?

True Leadership Principle: It almost goes without saying, but integrity is critical to trust and effective leadership. Because it is such an essential and challenging issue, it must be said anyway.

Article II

Have you ever been to a function or an event, or even been part of an organization, and tried to get something fixed or moving and no one seems to be responsible or in charge? Everyone says, "that's not up to me," or "that's not my responsibility." It's a very frustrating situation both for you and for those who don't feel they have the power to help you. Every situation needs a clear leader.

For a while I had a part-time job delivering pizzas. One night after dark, and during the evening rush, I was heading toward the door with a bag full of fresh hot pizzas on my way to deliver them when the guy who owned the coin shop next door came in holding his head with blood streaming down his face and tells me very calmly, "I've been shot." I immediately set down the bag of pizzas and start loudly barking orders. I call the store manager by name and shout, "You call 911 right now!" I take the bleeding man by the arm, lead him to the corner of the entryway and tell him, "Sit down right there!" I turn and look and see another driver, and calling her by name I say, "Bring me a big stack of paper napkins right now!" I then turn my attention back to the injured man and calmly start asking him questions about what happened, while checking how serious his head wound is and looking him over for other injuries. I keep asking him questions and keep him talking so that he will stay calm. He is in shock, but not too badly, so I keep him talking. I ask him to follow my finger with his eyes and he does so normally. I don't have anything to keep him warm but it's summertime and warm in the store so I don't think that's a big issue. His head wound is bleeding a lot as all head wounds do, but it appears to be just in the scalp and doesn't appear to have entered his skull. It looks like the bullet entered near the middle of his forehead and skittered along the skull without penetrating, exiting just above the hairline. He's bleeding and little shaky, but otherwise seems to be okay.

It turns out that a guy who had been coming into his store for a while looking at rare and valuable coins had walked into the store with a .38 caliber pistol and shot the shop owner right between the eyes. As the guy pulled the gun, the owner had jumped up and back, so the bullet entered at an angle, never penetrating his skull. He was still conscious but went down with the shot and had the presence of mind to play dead so the guy thought he had killed him. After the robber left the owner got up and came next door where I was the first person he saw.

About this time the EMTs come bursting through the door and over to where we are. I tell them what I did, what I noticed, and what his condition seems to be. They ask me a couple of quick questions and then turn their attention to the wounded man. I get up, go over and pick up my bag of pizzas, and go out the door, stepping past firetrucks and firemen, police and police cars, and reporters and news trucks. I then get into my car and head off to make my delivery.

True Leadership Principle: Someone has to be in charge and it's best if that person has leadership skills.

Because of my military and leadership training, because of the fact that I have first aid and basic emergency training, and because my automatic reaction in an emergency is to stay calm and collected, I was the perfect person to lead in this particular emergency situation. Basically, I'm the guy you want to have around when things get crazy, especially in a life-threatening way. I see what needs to be done and how to do it, then proceed to execute. I don't get scared, and I don't get flustered.

In an emergency, anyone who chooses to lead and has the skills can do so, but in ordinary day-to-day operations not having a clear idea of who is the leader is deadly to the continued survival of an organization. It's a clear sign of poor leadership.

So what about Article II? Article II establishes the Executive Branch of the government and lays out the framing of who the President is, who the President can and can't be, the duties and the powers of the President, how the President is elected, term of office, and how the President interacts with and relates to the other branches of the government, the states, and the people. Basically, this section is a detailed job description that lays out what the President of the United States can, must, and cannot do. This is pretty important considering he has the most powerful military in the world at his disposal as Commander-in-Chief, and many of his decisions are literally life or death decisions. There are job descriptions for the Representatives and the Senators in Article I and for the Supreme Court in Article III, but none are as detailed as those for the President in Article II. In fact, the longest clause in the entire Constitution is in Article II.

True Leadership Principle: Written, clear, and agreed upon job descriptions and expectations are essential to avoid misunderstandings that can damage credibility and trust.

While checks and balances between the various branches of government are written throughout the Constitution, they are most obvious here because Article II creates the most powerful person in the world. Since the Framers had just broken away from a king, they certainly did not want to create another one.

True Leadership Principle: The limits on a leader's authority must be clear and enforceable (and never violated by the leader) or credibility and trust are lost.

Article III

Imagine working in a situation where there is no ability to direct or enforce the rules. Worse yet, there is no way to protect yourself from being abused by someone bigger, stronger, richer, or whatever than you. What happens to fairness and trust in a situation like that? Now, I'm not suggesting that it's necessary to become totally rule-bound. That type of inflexibility kills creativity and fails to allow for individual circumstances and adjustments which are key to effective leadership. But it is important to have some rules that are clear and agreed upon by everyone involved.

True Leadership Principle: Some rules are necessary and a great leader will enforce them fairly as well as follow them.

The Judicial Branch was created by Article III to enforce the rules and to help keep the other two branches of government in check. Remember, the purpose of the government is to protect the rights of the people. The problem with power is that those with power almost always want to have more power. For that to happen, power has to come from those being led ("We the People" in the case of the government). Fairness dictates that we should only give more power away when there is a compelling need to do so and not at the whim of a "so-called" leader who just wants more power. The Framers created a beautiful frame here where each of the three branches has the ability to restrict the power of the other two. In other words, they are held accountable by each other.

True Leadership Principle: Accountability is critical to achieve optimum performance. It also keeps things on track.

Accountability partners are one of the most important things a great leader creates for themselves and for their people. Not only does that create checks and balances but it also creates incentive for all involved to do what they said they will, and to do it by a deadline. Another beauty of this process is that your accountability partners become a mastermind group with you. Masterminds tend to develop better answers, ideas, and solutions to problems than any individual leader, no matter how talented that person may be, can ever do by themselves.

True Leadership Principle: Great leaders seek out and enroll multiple accountability partners and mastermind groups both within and outside of their organizations.

Article IV

This article creates the frames that define the relationships between the states, as well as between the states and the federal government. This is very important. How difficult would it be if, every time you crossed a state line, you had to get a new driver's license for the state you were now driving in? What would that do, to not only your ability to travel freely, but your ability to do business outside of your own state?

I look at this frame as being kind of like the human resources department in a company. Human resources puts out all the various policy and procedure manuals. They also define the various benefits that all employees receive and administer those benefits in a fair and equitable way. They are responsible for hiring and firing so they have an enforcement role. They are basically responsible for making sure that all the interactions between departments (at least the interactions that are related to the people), all the people in the organization, and the organization itself are handled in a fair and orderly manner. Although this frame is kind of administrative in nature, it is absolutely necessary for the smooth and successful functioning of the organization or, in the case of Article IV, the government.

True Leadership Principle: The relationships between the organization and its various constituencies must be clearly

defined and fairly administered. This frame is kind of mundane but it is very important.

Article V

This article outlines how the Constitution may be amended. There are two ways to propose amendments: either Congress proposes amendments, or two-thirds of the states can call for a convention to propose amendments. In both cases, all amendments must be approved by three-fourths of the states before they become part of the Constitution. This is another great example of how a good frame creates a balance between competing interests and points of view without showing undue favor to either one.

In this case, the states are on equal footing with the federal congress to create clarification and necessary changes in structure. Because these types of changes are so impactful and far-reaching in their effects, the process was made very cumbersome so that no changes can be made too quickly. This way all perspectives are considered, and hopefully all foreseeable issues are accounted for. Also, since no one has the ability to predict the future, this process provides a way to adjust to changes in circumstances, technology, etc.

In the case of us as leaders in our various roles today, we need to be able to make adjustments in our own organizations as well. This applies to every type of organization, from a family to a government. Because things are changing so fast (primarily driven by changes in technology) we must be able to adjust to those changes just in order to survive, and if we want to thrive (which all great leaders want to do) we must continue to change and grow. We need processes that we can use to make the adjustments we need in order to thrive and to accomplish our visions and goals.

True Leadership Principle: Great leaders continually assess and adjust in order to anticipate and thrive.

Article VI
This article makes the Constitution the supreme law of the land. This means that if any state law conflicts with the Constitution, that state law will be invalid. It also states that federal officers must take an oath to support the Constitution much like the oath I took when I joined the US Air Force, which I stated at the beginning of this book. There are two essential objectives framed in this Article that apply to leadership.

First, there must be some overall reference point against which all activities can be measured. In the case of a business, that is often profitability. There are two problems with that. In the first place, profitability is a made up number that can be manipulated over a wide range. I've asked accountants in my classes many times about the following example and they always answer in agreement. Take the example of providing two income statements for the same company over the same time period but prepare them for different audiences. The first is for someone looking to buy the company and the second is for the IRS. In the first case, the statement will show the highest possible number for profit, and the second will show the lowest possible number. If they are prepared properly, both statements would pass an audit, although the profit numbers are very different! This means that profit is a made up number (within the limits of the rules of accounting). In most cases, it's better to use something else to measure performance instead of using a manufactured profit number. Things like customer satisfaction surveys, warranty return numbers, as well as other factors concerning quality and value are much better because they put the focus and incentives on the things that will guarantee long-term success. Of course, these things are harder to measure accurately and are more nebulous, but then that's true with everything leadership related.

True Leadership Principle: There must be a way to decide who and what has the final say and everyone must clearly understand what that is.

The second important frame is the idea of taking an oath of loyalty. In general loyalty in most things is assumed and expected, but in leadership situations such as these, a formal oath is required. Not only did I swear an oath to the Constitution when I joined the Air Force but I took an oath when I got married, was required to be sworn in when I was seated on a jury, and have had to attest to an oath in many other cases, like signing important documents. Taking an oath is a reminder that what you are doing is extremely important, and needs to be taken seriously.

True Leadership Principle: Great leaders are loyal to themselves, their principles, their people, and their organizations and expect loyalty from the people they lead in return. Two-way loyalty enhances trust.

Article VII

This article is very short and simply frames how many states had to accept the Constitution for it to be valid and enforced in those states. This simplicity is very deceptive because it utilizes one of the most powerful and important principles of great leadership –the buy-in. The process framed in this article allowed the people – through their elected state representatives – to buy-in to the whole concept of the Constitution, and to the Constitution itself.

Great leadership is not possible without the buy-in by everyone involved, beginning with the leader himself and including everyone else impacted by their leadership. Great leadership is about influence and invitation. It does not work under coercion. That's a management approach that never works long-term, and long-term is what great leadership is about. Remember, things can be effectively managed and forced but people cannot. Also, effective buy-in is not a one-time thing. Buy-in happens every day (sometimes multiple times a day).

In fact, buy-in is so important that we fought a war over it in which over 600,000 Americans lost their lives when some states decided to leave the Union. Buy-in and maintaining buy-in is pretty serious stuff! Of course, we don't usually go to war over buy-in's these days. We usually give them the chance to renew their buy-in, and if they choose not to we send them on their way. In the final analysis, leading people effectively is based on them voluntarily choosing to be led by you. That's a big responsibility, and a challenge since you will make mistakes – everyone does – and if those mistakes are serious, trust will be lost. Without trust, effective leadership is impossible.

True Leadership Principle: Buy-in is crucial! Getting and maintaining buy-in is one of the most important things that great leaders do.

THE AMENDMENTS: BOUNDARIES, GUARANTEES, AND CLARIFICATIONS

◆

If you are familiar with football –American football, not soccer – you know that each end of the field has a goalpost. While most points are scored by moving the ball across a line on the field (the goal line) by either passing or running the ball, the goalpost defines how points are scored through kicks. The goalpost is shaped like a block letter "U" (works for me since one of my degrees is from the University of Utah, otherwise known as "The U") which defines the bottom and two sides of a rectangle of unlimited height. As long as the ball passes through that rectangle as the result of a legal play, points are scored.

Here's the thing. The ball can pass through that invisible rectangle anywhere and the points scored are the same. It doesn't have to be in the center – anywhere is ok. It can even hit the side posts or the bottom cross post and as long as it somehow bounces through, it counts exactly the same as if it had been dead center. In other words, the kicker has the freedom to put the ball anywhere within the boundaries of that rectangle and it counts the same.

True Leadership Principle: Your people need to clearly understand what the boundaries are and to have complete freedom the operate anywhere within those boundaries.

The first ten amendments are known collectively as the Bill of Rights and they define the boundaries that the government must stay within. The difference between the rectangle defined by the football goalpost and the rectangle defined by the Constitution is the rectangle defined for the government has four clearly defined sides as opposed to three and an unlimited height defined by a football goalpost. This means that the government only has the freedom to operate anywhere within the box, but not outside that box. Everything outside that box is reserved to the states and to "We the People". The freedom to operate there does not belong to the Federal Government (see the Tenth Amendment).

True Leadership Principle: Leaders MUST clearly define the box that people are allowed the freedom to operate within. They MUST then allow themselves and their people that freedom. Leaders also MUST clearly, repeatedly, and consistently communicate limits of that box and the fact that people have the complete freedom to operate within it.

A great leader has no right to discipline anyone if what that person did is the result of poorly defined boundaries. That's the leader's fault, and it's the leader's responsibility to fix. What this means is that leaders also have a box that they cannot operate outside of. That box is usually a little different than the box of whoever is being led but it still exists and the leaders MUST remain within their boundaries of operations. In actuality, this is more critical for the leader than for the follower because leadership is based upon trust and if trust is violated (especially repeatedly) it is quickly lost and is almost impossible to regain.

True Leadership Principle: Great leadership is based upon trust.

The Bill of Rights also has a Preamble (otherwise known as a mission statement) that outlines the "why" for its existence. The relevant part of that Preamble reads:

"THE Conventions of a number of the States, having at the time of their adopting the Constitution, expressed a desire, in order to prevent misconstruction or abuse of its powers, that further declaratory and restrictive clauses should be added: And as extending the ground of public confidence in the Government, will best ensure the beneficent ends of its institution."

Here's what that means. The states (and the people through their state representatives) wanted to ensure that the framing of the Constitution would be locked in. After all, who would want a house that looks like a Picasso painting, but is so structurally unsound that it falls down when you slam the door? The Framers clearly did not want the government to abuse its powers. So, in the Bill of Rights they added specific definitions (declarations) and restrictions so that the government would not be allowed to infringe on the rights of the states, or the God-given rights of the people, beyond what was specifically defined. The Bill of Rights essentially better frames, more clearly defines, and tightens the box that the government has the freedom to operate within in order to protect the rights of both the states and the people.

True Leadership Principle: People thrive best when organizations have very tight, small, and clearly defined boxes that they must operate within and when people have very large boxes that they have the freedom to operate within. Ironically this arrangement is also the best way to insure that the organization will thrive and grow.

However counterintuitive this might seem it must be the case since this principle has worked in the United States for well over two hundred years, and counting. The proof of a true principle is its long-term staying power – remember the test of truth is: "it worked yesterday, it works today, and it will work tomorrow regardless of anyone's opinion about it".

True Leadership Principle: Boundaries can be negotiated, but once established must be respected. Boundaries can be renegotiated from time to time as needed just like the Constitution can be amended, but that process should be very deliberate and carefully used.

If you want to be a great leader you must establish, respect, and enforce your own boundaries and the boundaries of others. This creates safety, respect, and predictability which allows people to have the freedom to perform to the very best they are capable, and to continually expand their capabilities.

True Leadership Principle: Great leaders do not micro-manage! They teach true principles and let people operate independently using those principles.

There are many more things I could say about the true leadership principles in and around the Constitution of the United States but the ones I have included here are the most important, and should be incorporated into your personal constitution (i.e. who and what you are) if you want to be a great leader. Now let's look at how to do that.

Ideally governing and leading are almost the same thing. In the real world and as a practical matter they are too often almost diametrically opposed. Governing tends to be seen and practiced as forcing people to do things, where leading tends to be more like inviting people to follow. This is the cause of a huge problem because no one likes to be forced and when that happens people tend to resist in every possible way. If they can't resist overtly because they are afraid of the consequences, they will simply take it underground, become passive-aggressive and undermine the organization and leadership at every turn. The value that the organization has previously been able to create with its customers simply vanishes. If not corrected this will eventually lead to failure of the organization.

If leaders recognize this and address it effectively they will not only be able to save the organization, but can take it to a place where it will thrive. What great leaders do is to move themselves and everyone else they lead out of that coercive place and into the invitation only space. This opens up the freedom, creativity, and energy of the people in the organization and strengthens trust. With that trust and the needed freedom to act, people are able to do their jobs better, innovate, and make the changes required to deliver more effectively, and the results will be of higher quality. It changes the culture of the organization along with the practices, which makes everything run much more smoothly and progress more rapidly to the attainment of their goals and the realization of their vision.

True Leadership Principle: Great leaders practice motivation and influence by invitation. That is, they invite people to join them in their vision and their goals.

STEP 2:
DEFINE YOUR CONSTITUTION

❧

Incorporating the leadership principles related to "The Constitution" into "your constitution" as a leader.

What to learn:
Seeking and accepting responsibility – "if it's to be it's up to me"
Character development process
Conduct improvement process
Charisma enhancement process

What to avoid:
Quick fixes that never work long-term

So what's the point of all this? Well, nothing, unless we use these true principles to change ourselves and how we lead – use them to change our own personal constitutions. I have discovered that this isn't about changing everything about myself. After all, it would be foolish to "throw out the baby with the bath water" and give up my unique abilities that I can use to make the world better and impact people's lives for good. It's about accepting the responsibility to incorporate these principles into my character, my conduct, and my charisma to make me the best leader, and the best person, that I can be. Or, at the very least, move me further and faster along that path. In essence, the incorporation and practice of these principles enhance who I am, make me a better person and a better leader, accelerate my development, and quickly and continuously make me more effective and better able to help others.

The true leadership principles we have discussed so far in this book are found in and around the founding documents of the United States that the Framers used, but that is not the only place true leadership principles are found. For example, true leadership principles are contained in all the sacred books of all religions. They are also found in books like this written by many authors over the years.

While there is a priority in the three "Cs" –Character, Conduct, and Charisma– that doesn't mean that you should develop them in that sequence. You actually need to work on them all at once and develop them in parallel as you keep the priorities in mind. It's more about keeping in mind some very important attitudes which you will want to incorporate into your character. I have touched on some of these earlier but it's important to talk about them again as a reminder, or a frame, for making you a better leader. The first is responsibility – "if it's to be it's up to me." No one can improve your leadership except you. If I do pushups, you don't get stronger, I do. Each leader is responsible for his or her own self-leadership and their own development. Next, you have to have faith in the process and faith in yourself. You need to believe that you can do it and that it will work for you. Remember here that true principles work everywhere, and since this development of your leadership is based upon true principles it will work for you, but only if you work it consistently enough and long enough. It has worked and still works for me, so it will work for you too. We are not that different from one another.

True Leadership Principle: If I can do it, you can do it, because we really aren't that different from one another.

Another critical attitude is commitment. You have to be committed to developing yourself and your leadership, so much so that you will never give up. You are never beaten if you never quit. I always say that commitment is like breakfast. The chicken is a contributor but the pig is committed. I suggest you be like the pig in that sense. An attitude that does well with commitment is persistence. I made the decision that I would either develop my leadership skills or die trying. In fact, once I understood what that meant a little better I actually made the decision to continue developing my leadership skills until the day I die. I made a lifestyle choice.

True Leadership Principle: Great leadership begins with understanding you need to develop it, committing to do so, and persisting in that commitment.

A word here about attitudes. My attitude is not about what has happened, is happening, or will happen to me.

My attitude is about a conscious decision that I make daily regarding how I will think about and process what has happened, is happening, or will happen to me. Attitude is a choice. William James said, "The greatest discovery of my generation is that a human being can alter his life by altering his attitudes." He is absolutely right about that, and I'm living proof. I have a sister who has spent her career as a social worker and professional counselor and she has told me more than once that I have changed over my life more than anybody else she knows. How have I done that? By making and keeping commitments to myself and others about my attitudes. It works! In fact, maybe my next book should be called, "The Attitude of a Great Leader." Who knows? Anything's possible. Remember, this book is not about me. It's about you, me, and all of us improving our leadership skills day by day. I'm just telling you how it works, and I know it does from my own experience.

True Leadership Principle: Great leadership requires developing and maintaining great attitudes.

The next thing to understand is that you cannot develop great leadership skills without a mentor. In fact, it takes a lot of mentors. Because leadership is learned experientially you must learn by experiencing the knowledge of your mentors. This is done through their books, audios, webinars, whatever you can get your hands on, as well as from face-to-face interaction. Management can be learned intellectually for the most part, but leadership must be developed experientially. Think about it. You can see and measure a good manager but you FEEL great leaders and leadership. Leadership is not even experienced intellectually, so it certainly can't be learned that way.

True Leadership Principle: Great leadership is felt, learned, and practiced emotionally and experientially – not intellectually. It requires a shift from your head to your heart – from what you think to what you feel.

Remember the six men of Indostan? Well, you need to become all six and eventually sixty more in order to understand and incorporate the "leadership elephant" into your constitution. To develop your own leadership skills, you have to experience every bit of that elephant that you possibly can. That's where mentors come in. Ronald Regan said, "Each generation goes further than the generation preceding it because it stands on the shoulders of that generation. You will have opportunities beyond anything we've ever known." Working with mentors is a way of standing on the shoulders of those who have walked the road of great leadership before you. Based upon their own unique experiences and perspectives, each mentor is an expert and has a special focus on one part of the elephant. So don't just read this book. Read every book related to leadership that you can find. Don't just read my books but listen to my audios, watch my videos, listen to my interviews on radio, TV, and podcasts. Come to my seminars, courses, and programs. Bring me in to speak, coach, and train your people and so on. But don't just do this with me. Do the same thing with every leader and leadership expert you can. This will allow you to develop your own, personal, unique leadership style. If you don't relate to me then go learn from someone else, but learn as much as you can from as many experts as you can as often, continuously, and rapidly as you can. You've only got one life so don't waste it. Don't die with your leadership music still in you!

True Leadership Principle: Great leaders find, work with, and learn from great mentors.

While we're on the subject of elephants, don't allow yourself to get overwhelmed by all this. You know how you eat an elephant don't you? One bite at a time! So just keep taking bites, chewing them thoroughly, and swallowing them. Then take another bite and repeat. I've been practicing this for decades and I can promise you that if you tackle things this way, you will eventually see progress. Then at some point you will be able to look back ten, twenty, or even more years and be able to say, "Wow! I actually have come a long way!"

True Leadership Principle: Great leaders move forward continuously one small step at a time. They understand the value of process.

You need to think of yourself as a leader. The reality is that you truly are a leader – everyone is (good or bad) – so I suggest you think of yourself as a good leader. That's actually another very important attitude related to accountability. You see, if you are always thinking of yourself as a leader you will start thinking that people are looking to you and watching you (which they always are by the way). But if you think of yourself like that – essentially that you are always on stage, always in the spotlight, and always needing to set an example – you will act like a better leader and develop the habits of a great leader. Essentially, you are enlisting everyone you meet and allowing them to hold you accountable. And, as we all know, we always perform better if we are going to be held to account for our actions. This gives you help, increases transparency, and speeds the progress of your development.

True Leadership Principle: Great leaders enlist multiple accountability partners and utilize them to hold themselves accountable constantly.

Finally, you must practice, practice, and practice! Every time you learn something new or have a new insight, go try it out and see how it works. Then assess how well it worked or didn't work, adjust based upon the reality of that feedback and try it out again. Always remember that great leadership is developed experientially, and you cannot develop anything experientially without experiencing it! That seems pretty obvious but we are conditioned from kindergarten through graduate school that we learn things intellectually. The reality is that intellectual learning is generally the worst way to learn something, and is only barely better than not learning it at all! In fact, you really don't learn much of anything intellectually. I mean, did you ever take calculus, or physics, or English literature, or whatever in school? If you haven't used it a lot since then how much do you remember? In fact, how much did you remember, or even care, a month after you took the final and got your grade? Intellectual learning really doesn't work well, does it? I remember more than once walking out of a final and mentally pulling the handle to flush it out of my mind! In fact, in some cases I remember actually acting out the flushing motion with my hand beside my head!

True Leadership Principle: Great leadership comes experientially from practice. Great leaders practice great leadership every day.

As a final reinforcement of this let, me list the steps to "The Fix." These steps will help you close the leadership gap, so now you can quickly copy them and take them with you to remind yourself what you need to do to keep yourself on track.

The Fix

1. Learn and frequently review the true principles of great leadership.

2. Believe that you can grow and become a better leader.

3. Accept the responsibility - keep in mind the vision, the goals, and the benefits, then commit and persist in the development process.

4. Improve and control your attitudes.

5. Remember leadership is experienced, so it must be learned experientially. Go and experience it every day.

6. Find, work with, and learn from mentors. Choose mentors wisely.

7. Keep eating the leadership elephant – one bite at a time.

8. Enlist and utilize as many accountability partners as you can.

9. Practice, practice, practice – remember perfect practice makes perfect permanent.

Remember, there is no fast and easy way to become a great leader – no quick fix. Working with mentors is the only shortcut there is, and it is the only shortcut you absolutely need to take. You certainly will not live long enough to experience everything yourself, so learn from others! This process has been going on for thousands of years and is still unfolding. You can be a unique and irreplaceable part of that unfolding masterpiece if you choose, starting from right where you are today. So this is my invitation to you. Come join the party. Impact and improve the world with your own unique mix of gifts, experience, insights, and leadership. If you don't do that, the world will be a little less rich and vital because no one can replace your uniqueness – what only you can contribute will forever be absent. What a tragedy that would be! So I invite you to "Suck it up, Buttercup!" and become a vital part of the solution – good luck!

Epilogue

"Mind what you have learned. Save you it can!"
—Yoda

So here they are – the true leadership principles within the Constitution, specifically the ones I decided to incorporate into my own constitution, as a person. Here's the thing. I don't know it all, no one does, but I keep learning a little bit more each day about that elephant called Leadership, and I invite you to do the same and join me on this journey. There is a song written by Hal David and Burt Bacharach that was first recorded by Jackie DeShannon in 1965, it goes, "What the world needs now is love, sweet love..." and while that's clearly true, what is needed much more are great leaders. There is a lot more love sweet love in the world than there are great leaders and, without more great leaders and leadership, love sweet love will grow dimmer and may even flicker and go out. That would be both tragic and catastrophic. The results of that, if it happens, will be enormous. Beyond comprehension for individuals, families, businesses, governments, other organizations, and the entire world. I don't want to see that happen, so that is why I do what I do. I'm working to help the world by developing more great leaders in the world – starting with myself. I don't know if I'm a great leader yet. There are some who think I am, but I'm not so sure. However, I intend to be and expect to be someday and I know that if I continue to develop myself and help develop other great leaders, eventually I will become a great leader myself. I do know that I am much further down the road than I used to be so I know from my own experience that this process works. I invite you to join me. Believe you can become a great leader if you will put in the effort to do so, because you can. That's the beautiful thing about human beings. We can become just about anything if we put in the effort for a long enough time. I'm excited for you and I'm excited for myself – let's do this!

One more story...

There once was a little boy who wasn't treated very well. That's a bit of an understatement. Actually, he was abused daily and in every imaginable way. Being the oldest child he was told that he was responsible for the behavior of his younger siblings and was beaten whenever anything went wrong, which was every day, usually many times. He was abused and neglected by those who should have been his champions. He was smart enough to do well in school (of course he was beaten if he didn't), but had few social skills and almost no real friends, was physically smaller than those in his class because he was younger than they were, and was bullied constantly. The one good friend he had in grade school died in an accident when he was eleven years old, leaving the little boy with no real friends once more. The physical abuse stopped late in junior high when the little boy finally grew big and strong enough to overpower his primary abuser, his mother, but the other types of abuse–the isolation, and the bullying– continued. His grades dropped significantly.

Then when he was sixteen, something life changing happened that altered his trajectory from one that could have led him to prison, an early death, or even to becoming a school shooter. His family moved from the old small town to a new small town over one hundred miles away. The boy had an insight (he thought it was inspiration) and he realized that this move was his opportunity for a new, fresh start since no one there had ever heard of him before. He would be starting with a clean slate. So he made the decision that things would be different, be better, and he committed to make the most of this opportunity. His fear that this might be his last chance just poured gasoline on the fire of his commitment, and he knew he had to make it work this time. He knew he had to step out and make a bunch of friends. He knew he had to stop the bullying before it got started at his new school. He didn't know exactly how to do this so he prayed for guidance and strength and stepped into the unknown. What he didn't realize at the time was that he had just decided to become a leader and committed to improve his leadership skills every day for the rest of his life.

So that's what he did. He chose to act friendly and to initiate conversations with others, and to his surprise they liked him and were friendly in return. The bullying never returned as he started a growth spurt during that first year and was soon over six feet tall. His grades improved to the point that he actually graduated with honors two years later. While these changes happened, he still struggled with an abusive and chaotic home life among other personal issues. There's a saying that goes, "If you remember the 60's you weren't there!" so I'll leave that part of the story to your imagination. There was a bad first marriage and an ugly divorce, joining the Air Force in lieu of being drafted into the Army or Marines during the Vietnam War due to a low draft lottery number, the ups and downs of education, business success and failure, family and other challenges, and the journey continues today. It's not like everything was instantly wonderful but a new course and direction had been set.

And now he has written this book for you...

Here's the point. When I say if I can do it you can do it, I'm not kidding. I absolutely know that anybody can become the leader they were meant to be if they will pay the price, because I have done it and continue to do it every day. You can do it too. Just choose, act, and enjoy the journey. All the best!

True Leadership Principle: When a challenge comes great leaders first deal with it, then adjust to it, and finally embrace it and use it to help make themselves and others better.

Appendix

List of True Leadership Principles discussed in this book.

Great leaders enhance their charisma by telling engaging stories constantly.

Great answers are found by asking great questions. If you want to improve the quality of your answers you must improve the quality of the questions you are asking.

Great character is the foundation. Without great character, great leadership is not possible and your leadership will always fail eventually! There are only a few absolute barriers in life (i.e. things that restrict you from achievement), and this is one of that select group. If you want to lead effectively you MUST develop great character!

Conduct flows from character.

Great leaders listen to understand, not to rebut or comment.

Great leaders are consistent and predictable, but not inflexible, boring, or overbearing.

Great leaders focus on what they do best and hire the rest.

Great leaders are humble. Humble means teachable.

Nothing good can ever be accomplished without some risk.

Charisma is 7% Communication with words and 93% Presence (communicating non-verbally). To be effective a great leader must develop and use their Charisma.

Great Leaders have courage – especially social courage as part of their Character.

Wisdom helps you make good decisions. Wisdom is gained by making bad decisions!

Perfect practice makes perfect permanent.

All leaders are speakers, and all speakers are leaders.

Great leaders have a burning desire to move forward and an absolute belief that they can always find a way to do so.

Framing is one of the most crucial leadership principles every leader must develop and practice constantly.

All great leaders treat people fairly and respectfully, and never attempt to violate people's inherent rights. If a leader violates these rights they will lose trust and never be able to lead effectively.

You must enroll yourself first and keep yourself enrolled before you can effectively enroll others and keep them enrolled.

Self-leadership is the first leadership skill you must develop, practice, constantly improve, and maintain if you want to be a great leader.

Seeing the vision, yourself, is useless, unless and until you can successfully communicate it to others and enroll them in that vision.

All decisions are emotionally based! That's just how humans work!

Charismatic communication is an absolutely essential leadership skill that must be constantly practiced, used, and improved every day of your life if you want to be an effective, and possibly even a great, leader.

Leadership skills are the most powerful of all the skill sets.

Everyone leads at some point, so developing leadership skills is important to, and helps, everyone.

Great leaders are constantly working to align people's incentives with the long-term goals and vision.

Solid character is the foundation that makes leadership legitimate.

Quick-fix, "knee-jerk" solutions rarely work long-term and are poor leadership practice.

Great leaders do not care who gets the credit and wise leaders spread the credit around.

Great leaders know it's better to be good than to look good.

If you can't lead yourself, you can't lead others effectively. As you learn to lead yourself more effectively you will be able to lead others more effectively.

Responsibility is a gift and taking responsibility is a leader's gift to the world.

Great leaders NEVER give up!

Great leaders are great because they are constantly learning, gaining understanding, and practicing great leadership.

All things rise and fall based on the quality of the leadership – you, your family, your business, and your nation.

True leadership principles are timeless.

Every organization needs a mission statement to lay out the basic frames of the organization and its purpose. All involved people need to buy-in to that mission statement.

People need to feel they have a voice and an impact on decisions – either directly, by someone who represents their interests and their point of view, or both.

Compromise is often the best tactic and most desirable course of action. It often leads to better answers, tactics, and approaches due to the mastermind principle (essentially, two or more heads are better than one).

Not everything is open to compromise. For example, no matter how many legislators a state has each legislator only gets one vote. Changing that item was never included in the compromise. In other words, they did not make "some pigs more equal than others" to paraphrase George Orwell.

Great leadership requires two-way trust. The leader must trust their people and the people being led must trust the leader.

To say that integrity is critical to trust and effective leadership almost goes without saying, but because it is such an essential and challenging issue it must be said anyway.

Someone has to be in charge and it's best if that person has leadership skills.

Written, clear, and agreed upon job descriptions and expectations are essential to avoid misunderstandings that can damage credibility and trust.

The limits on a leader's authority must be clear and enforceable (and never violated by the leader) or credibility and trust are lost.

Some rules are necessary and a great leader will enforce them fairly, as well as follow them.

Accountability is critical to achieve optimum performance. It also keeps things on track.

Great leaders seek out and enroll multiple accountability partners and mastermind groups from both within and outside of their organizations.

The relationships between the organization and its various constituencies must be clearly defined and fairly administered. This frame is kind of mundane but it is very important.

Great leaders continually assess and adjust in order to anticipate and thrive.

There must be a way to ensure who and what has the final say, and everyone must clearly understand what that is.

Great leaders are loyal to themselves, their principles, their people, and their organizations and expect loyalty from the people they lead in return. Two-way loyalty enhances trust.

Buy-in is crucial! Getting and maintaining buy-in is one of the most important things that great leaders do.

Your people need to clearly understand what the boundaries are, and must have complete freedom to operate anywhere within those boundaries.

Leaders MUST clearly define the box that people are allowed the freedom to operate within. They MUST then allow themselves and their people that freedom.

Leaders also MUST clearly, repeatedly, and consistently communicate limits of that box and the fact that people have the complete freedom to operate within that box.

Great leadership is based upon trust.

People thrive best when organizations have very tight, small, and clearly defined boxes that they must operate within, and when people have very large boxes that they have the freedom to operate within. Ironically this arrangement is also the best way to guarantee that the organization will thrive and grow.

Boundaries can be negotiated, but once established must be respected. Boundaries can be renegotiated from time to time as needed just like the Constitution can be amended, but that process should be very deliberate and carefully used.

Great leaders do not micromanage! They teach true principles and let people operate independently using those principles.

Great leaders practice motivation and influence by invitation. That is, they invite people to join them in their vision and their goals.

If I can do it, you can do it because we really aren't that different from one another.

Great leadership begins with understanding you need to develop it, commiting to do so, and persisting in that commitment.

Great leadership requires developing and maintaining great attitudes.

Great leadership is felt, learned, and practiced emotionally and experientially – not intellectually. It requires a shift from your head to your heart – from what you think to what you feel.

Great leaders find, work with, and learn from great mentors.

Great leaders move forward continuously, one small step at a time. They understand the value of process.

Great leaders enlist multiple accountability partners and utilize them to hold themselves accountable constantly.

Great leadership comes from experiential practice. Great leaders practice great leadership every day.

When a challenge comes great leaders first deal with it, then adjust to it, and finally embrace it and use it to help make themselves, and others, better.

www.ingramcontent.com/pod-product-compliance
Lightning Source LLC
Chambersburg PA
CBHW071709210326
41597CB00017B/2411